SECRET
NEW YORK

SECRET
NEW YORK

The Unique Guidebook to New York's Hidden Sites, Sounds, & Tastes

Robert Sietsema

WITH PHOTOGRAPHS BY
Linda Rutenberg

ECW PRESS

The publication of *Secret New York* has been generously supported by the Government of Canada through the Book Publishing Industry Development Program.

CANADIAN CATALOGUING IN PUBLICATION DATA

Sietsema, Robert
Secret New York : the unique guidebook
to New York's hidden sites, sounds, & tastes

ISBN 1-55022-374-7

1. New York (N.Y.) – Guidebooks.   1. Title.

FC128.18.S547 1999   917.47'0443   C96-930700-2

Design and imaging by ECW *Type & Art*, Oakville, Ontario.
Printed by Imprimerie Interglobe Inc., Beauceville, Québec.

Distributed in Canada by General Distribution Services,
325 Humber College Blvd., Etobicoke, Ontario M9W 7C3.

Distributed in the United States by Login Publishers Consortium,
1436 West Randolph Street, Chicago, Illinois, U.S.A. 60607.

Published by ECW PRESS,
2120 Queen Street East, Suite 200, Toronto, Ontario M4E 1E2.

www.ecw.ca/press

PRINTED AND BOUND IN CANADA

TABLE OF CONTENTS

INTRODUCTION

By its nature, New York City is random and chaotic. This guide sets out to harness those qualities. Rather than systematically combing every neighborhood for its predictable major and minor sights, replicating the efforts of every previous guide, it sets out to locate what is most exciting about Gotham, leaping like a hyperactive child from topic to topic. In doing so, it encourages a different type of tourism. You won't find us recommending the Statue of Liberty, Rockefeller Center, or Times Square; this would turn a multidimensional city into a series of dog-eared postcards. In fact, we warn you away from tourist traps. Instead, we recommend activities that allow you to merge with the locals and come away feeling like you really know the city.

We invite you, for example, to visit an African neighborhood in Harlem, shop in the outdoor market, and enjoy a lunch of cheb, the national dish of Senegal. We invite you to stroll the boardwalk at Coney Island, taking in the sea vistas, dining at a Russian sidewalk café, and riding the last remaining big roller coaster in the city. We invite you to the rock clubs where local bands play and the underground sex shows where burlesque mixes easily with performance art. We direct you to museums with enthralling collections that are nearly empty and charge no admission instead of the places where you have to wait in long lines, pay an arm and a leg, and then crane your neck to see anything.

This guide will also save you money with up-to-date transportation tips that the other guides can't give you because their absentee staffs don't ride the subway every day. We tell you how to get discounts on museum admissions, and give hints on how to find a hotel that charges less than $150, a bed-and-breakfast for under $80, or a hostel for around $20. We tell you where the public restrooms are. *Secret New York* also teaches you how to relax in the city, enjoying its hidden parks, leisure activities, and church gardens. So go fly a kite. Or skate on a year-round ice rink. Or eat Korean food at four in the morning. When your visit's over, you'll be a New Yorker.

HOW TO USE
SECRET NEW YORK

This book is organized by topic rather than geographically. The best way to approach it is to browse according to what interests you the most. If you're a chocolate fiend, begin with the Secret Chocolate section; if you can't wait to hit the subway but can't figure out how to use the new fare card, turn to Secret Metrocard. One of the most useful sections is Secret Periodicals, which recommends publications — many of them free — that New Yorkers use to find out what's happening on a day-by-day basis. Another important section is Secret Maps, which helps you acquire the tools to find your way around the city with confidence.

For every attraction we provide an address and phone number. We don't clutter the presentation with hours of operation (which often change); cross streets; subway, bus, and driving directions; or prices, unless they're remarkable in some way. Accordingly, we encourage you to phone ahead to find out this information and also to confirm that a place is still open. Real-estate conditions in the city are harsh, and even though we've tried to choose durable attractions, some closings will inevitably occur before you get your hands on this volume.

Unless otherwise noted, all telephone numbers are within the 212 area code.

SECRET
AFRICAN

No American city can match New York in the size or scope of its African community. Eight years ago there was no visible African presence, but soon afterwards Senegalese and Ghanaians began to arrive — the former on student visas that permitted a six-month stay, allowing them to quickly establish street businesses. Selling counterfeit watches (see *Secret Watches)* and other portable, easily salable merchandise, they returned home at the end of six months with a tidy sum of cash. Many have come back again. The Ghanaians appeared at about the same time and obtained more permanent immigration arrangements; many have found work as taxi drivers.

Drawn by the burgeoning communities of Senegalese and Ghanaians, other West Africans began to arrive. French speakers tended to settle in the vicinity of West 116th Street between Malcolm X and Frederick Douglass, attracted by the **Malcolm Shabazz Mosque** (102 West 116th Street, 662-2200) and by a halal butcher — necessities for the mainly Islamic immigrants. The open-air **African market** at 116th and Malcolm X (aka Lenox Avenue) is one of the neighborhood's anchors, and one of the city's "must see" sights. Vendors peddle curios and apparel from all over West Africa, including Niger River mud cloth, conical Fulani hats of straw and leather, colorful shirts of handwoven material, and bolts of beautiful batik fabric, in addition to knockoffs of western merchandise like Tommy Hilfiger clothing and hip-hop cassettes.

For a bite to eat try **Africa Restaurant** (247 West 116th Street, 666-9400), where the Senegalese specialties run to cheb, a sauté of stuffed fish and vegetables over orange rice, and mafe, a stew of chicken or lamb in a thick peanut sauce. There's another branch of the same restaurant within a stone's throw of the **Theater District** (346 West 53rd Street, 399-7166). On the same 116th Street strip, **Kaloum** (126 West 116th Street, 864-2485) offers fare from Guinea, like sauce de feuilles, a beef stew thickened with a flavorful green sludge of potato leaves, in addition to a handful of Senegalese dishes, as all restaurants along this strip do to attract Senegalese diners in addition to their own countrypeople. As the name suggests, **Mali-Bo** (218 West 116th Street, 665-4481) slings Malian hash, such as tô, a millet porridge that can be paired with a variety of tomato and palm-oil sauces.

Ghanaians and other Anglophone Africans settled in the University Heights section of the Bronx and in Brooklyn's Flatbush, a mainly Caribbean neighborhood (see Secret Flatbush). In the Bronx, **Ebe Ye Yie** (2364 Jerome Avenue, Bronx, 718-563-6034) serves multiple varieties of fufu (mashed sweet potato or other tuber) with sauce, and wachei, a mixture of black-eyed peas and rice that's the forerunner of American hoppin' john. Ghanaian provender is also available in Manhattan near Columbia University at **Obaa Koryoe** (3151 Broadway, 316-2950). Also on the English-speaking side of the fence is **Demu Café** (773 Fulton Street, 718-875-8484), a Nigerian establishment in Fort Greene, one of Brooklyn's nicest neighborhoods.

Another quintessential African institution is **West Africa Grocery** (524 Ninth Avenue, 695-6215) in Hell's Kitchen, where all sorts of curious products are for sale. The *Village Voice* Web site (www.villagevoice.com/eats) provides an exhaustive list of African restaurants in the city, penned by yours truly.

SECRET

ALL-YOU-CAN-EAT

✤

New York seems bizarrely expensive to most visitors. One way to economize is by snacking continuously, but only downing one full meal per day — and making it an all-you-can-eat. Here are a few places to indulge a bottomless appetite.

At lunch, many Indian restaurants offer buffets. **Mitali West** (296 Bleecker Street, 989-1367) has a good one, but at $7.95 weekdays it's also one of the more expensive. Even better is Soho's **Karahi** (508 Broome Street, 965-1515), where $6.95 gets you a choice of over a dozen dishes, with flesh choices not limited to chicken as they are at many similar buffets. Midtown's **Chola** (232 East 58th Street, 688-0464) makes a similar offer, although the selection is disappointing compared with their far-flung regional menu. **Bay Leaf** (49 West 56th Street, 957-1818), in the vicinity of Columbus Circle, is pricier ($13.95), but the selection is broader and somewhat more delicately spiced. You can whittle these prices down to $5.95 or less by watching for Indian neighborhood restaurants, which often tempt passersby with all-you-can-eat deals, especially on the Upper West Side and in Chelsea. If you're willing to go to the Indian part of Jackson Heights (see Secret Indian), you'll find many luncheon buffets on 74th Street and 37th Avenue, just steps from the E, F, 7, and R trains.

Shiki's (69 Seventh Avenue South, 206-7024) is well known for its $17.95 sushi special, which includes unlimited maki and nigiri sushi. However, all of the unlimited sushi places around town impose annoying rules, and there's often a fine if you share with a fellow diner, leave a piece or two on your plate, or don't eat the complimentary salad.

If you want tons of meat, go to one of the rodizios. These Brazilian barbecues, which attained instant popularity a few years ago, feature gaucho-clad waiters who carry grilled meats around the dining room on skewers. You can have as much or as little as you like from a selection that often includes several types of steaks, lamb ribs, sweetbreads, and — gasp! — chicken hearts. The trick is to seek out the ones that actually use charcoal in their grills rather than gas. **Green Field** (108-01 Northern Boulevard, 718-672-5202) in Corona, Queens, is the most fun, but Manhattan's **Churrascaria Plataforma** (316 West 49th Street, 245-0505) has marginally better meats and a humongous salad bar, which will come as a relief to your not-so-hot-on-meat dining companions.

Cabana Carioca (123 West 45th Street, 581-8088) furnishes a sumptuous Brazilian/Portuguese buffet at lunchtime, with a cheaper price on the third floor ($6.95) than on the first ($9.95). The **Delegates Dining Room** at the United Nations has an incomparable unlimited spread at lunch (see Secret United Nations). For excellent all-you-can-swallow soul food, **Charles' Southern** (2837 Eighth Avenue, 926-4313) serves up ribs, collards, oven-barbecued chicken, and mac and cheese for $6.95 at lunch and $9.95 at dinner in a corner of Harlem where you won't see another tourist for as long as you linger there. It's very highly recommended, as is the unlimited vegetarian feed at **Vatan** (see Secret Gujarati Village).

SECRET

ALSO KNOWN AS

✤

Though it's signposted "Avenue of the Americas" throughout its length, locals insist on using the thoroughfare's previous name, Sixth

Avenue — and you should too. In Harlem, Eighth Avenue becomes Frederick Douglass, Seventh becomes Adam Clayton Powell, and Sixth becomes Malcolm X. "The East Village" was a coinage of real-estate speculators who wanted to imbue that neighborhood with the desirability of Greenwich Village. Traditionally, it was known as the Lower East Side. The original name of Kennedy Airport was Idlewild. The presidential-sounding Roosevelt Island, before it became an upscale development, was home to lunatic asylums and terminal-disease hospitals. Its previous moniker was Welfare Island (see Secret Tramway). Though city planners have tried to erase the Irish-working-class stigma of the neighborhood on the far-west side of Manhattan in the 30s and 40s by renaming it Clinton, the old name of Hell's Kitchen has stuck.

And, in spite of the Metropolitan Transportation Authority's attempts to create an integrated system of numbers, letters, and colors for the subway lines, many of the original train names persist, especially among old-timers. The F train in Brooklyn is still referred to as the Culver Local, the 7 as the Flushing train, and the 4, 5, and 6 as the Lexington Avenue Line.

SECRET

AMERICAN INDIANS

⚘

Everyone knows the story of how Dutchman Peter Minuit bought Manhattan from the Indians in 1626 for $40 worth of glass beads and went on to establish the town of New Amsterdam at its southern tip. People still chuckle at the story, but maybe the Indians didn't drive such a bad bargain after all — beads were a form of currency,

and they may have laughed all the way to the bead bank. For millennia, members of Delaware tribes speaking a dialect known as Munsee had used the island mainly as a preserve for hunting and foraging, finding better places in the metropolitan area to establish settlements. Several locales still retain their Munsee names: Rockaway (sandy place), Canarsie (grassy place), and, my favorite, Maspeth (bad water place), a town in Queens that sits on the north bank of Newtown Creek, an industrialized waterway that still richly deserves its Indian name.

Other than gazing at the map, you can get in touch with Indian culture by visiting the Smithsonian's **American Indian Museum** (1 Bowling Green, 668-6624), the repository of a motherlode of Native American artifacts representing tribes from Florida to Alaska. The museum occupies the Federal-period Custom House, a magnificent structure that strikes the correct note of respect for the vast collections. For a more pan-American take on the subject, check out the overcrowded-on-the-weekends **American Museum of Natural History** (79th Street and Central Park West, 769-5100), a massive pile founded by Teddy Roosevelt overlooking the park. In addition to North American artifacts, the galleries also feature Mayan, Aztec, and Incan pieces, including lots of hammered-gold objects from Mexico and Central America.

The American Indian Museum has an impressive gift shop, but if you want to browse Native American collectibles in a big way, visit **Common Ground** (113 West 10th Street, 989-4178), a store where, the clerk assured me, 95% of the merchandise is made by Indian craftspeople (the balance is Southwestern bric-a-brac, like strings of chili lights). The store stocks Zuni fetishes, turquoise jewelry, beaded moccasins, Navajo blankets, dorky bola ties, animal-skin drums, and feathered headdresses much too big, and maybe too embarrassing, to display in your home. For the lowdown on Indian activities occurring in the metropolitan area, many open to non-Indians, contact the **American Indian Community House** (404 Lafayette Street, 598-0100).

The best Indian experience, though, involves no expenditure of money. Take the A train to the 207th Street stop and walk two blocks west to **Inwood Hill Park**. Thread your way through the handball courts till you see a paved path that climbs the escarpment as it goes north. Follow it to the top of the hill, cross the meadow, and follow another path that descends on the other side, again in a northerly direction. After a few twists and turns, you'll come to a series of shallow caves in a rock wall to which you may ascend if you do some modest rock climbing. Archeologists have discovered evidence that they were used as hunting shelters by various tribes. As you crouch in the caves and look down at an expanse of near wilderness that contains the last remnants of Manhattan's primeval forest, you'll see the island as the Indians saw it 400 years ago.

SECRET ANGLOPHILIA

Barley water, bangers, steak and kidney pie, Cumberland sausage, wine gums, crisps — if you know what these things are, or want to find out, **Myers of Keswick** (634 Hudson Street, 691-4194) is your place. This wee grocery had its origins in an English Lake District town and carries many unique items found in few other places. On the downside there's All Day Dinner, a type of canned baked beans that features bacon, sausage, and egg-stuffed pork balls in a tomato gravy, but on the upside is a vast selection of daily and weekly newspapers, and tons of candy, snack food, and soda, as well as a beer/lemonade admixture. The glory of the shop, however, are the English pastries baked on the premises and sold hot from the oven all day long. Crane your neck over the refrigerator counter to see what's cooling on the sideboard and order accordingly. My favorites are Cornish pasties; potato, cheddar, and onion pies; and Scotch eggs. They'll heat anything that isn't currently hot, but it's not the same.

Tea and Sympathy (108 Greenwich Avenue, 807-8329) is a café that offers afternoon tea with accoutrements like scones, finger sandwiches, and clotted cream. It's also a favorite spot for Anglophilic lunch and dinner. Next door is a newly opened affiliated shop that sells teapots, ornate and plain, and features one of the city's better selections of teas, biscuits, and cakes.

The **English Speaking Union** (16 East 69th Street, 879-6800) hosts speakers, courses, and exhibits at their townhouse on the Upper East Side, and most of their programs are open to the public. A reasonable yearly membership fee of $80 allows you use of the facilities, including a library, and reduced admission to events. You'll also get a discount on the afternoon tea dispensed every weekday afternoon beginning at three.

For an English-style pub, check out **North Star** (93 South Street, 509-6757) or **Scratcher** (209 East 5th Street, 477-0030), where the bar is decorated with tins of Cadbury Cocoa and Marmite and a pub lunch is provided. And for English contemporary dance music at its drone-on best, try dropping in on Friday nights at **Vanity** (28 East 23rd Street, 254-6117), where GBH (Great British House) fills the room.

S E C R E T

AROMATHERAPY

✤

Aromatherapy, the lately invented art of influencing one's mental and physical health via the olfactory organ, is being touted everywhere nowadays: in the manifold shops that purvey bath needs (see Secret Bath), in department stores like Macy's, and in the Gap and other chain haberdasheries. But, if you wish to indulge, why not pick a shop that specializes in this arcane pseudoscience? **Enfleurage** (321 Bleecker Street, 691-1610) supplies all your aromatherapy needs, from candles to powdered incense to essential oils mixed to your specifications and priced in the $10-to-$20 range. Gift givers will appreciate the $39.95 starter kit, handsomely boxed and stocked with aloe vera, bath salts, candles, and eight essential oils to create different moods, with a rudimentary heat diffuser to launch them noseward.

S E C R E T

ATMs

✤

One thing about the Big Apple — you won't have any trouble getting cash from the automatic teller machines no matter where you come from. New York's ATMS are among the most versatile and accommodating in the world, and you can find several per block in some of the wealthier neighborhoods. Ask a local, "Where's the nearest cash machine?" and chances are you'll get a quick and convenient response. If you're cheap, like me, seek out the machines at **Citibank** and **Chase Manhattan**, which are the most profuse and don't tack on any surcharge for giving out money. Many other machines, including those found in supermarkets and convenience stores, will charge you $1 for the privilege of withdrawing cash. The worst machines are those of the Dime Savings Bank, which bilk you for $1.50.

S E C R E T
BAGELS

New York's most famous food is the bagel, brought to the city by Jewish immigrants in the nineteenth century. It's a ring of high-gluten dough that's first boiled for 45 seconds and then baked. This results in a characteristically tough exterior and chewy interior that's the perfect breakfast wake-up. It's also the city's quintessential between-meal snack — cheap and filling, whether eaten plain or toasted, spread with butter or cream cheese. Many New Yorkers prefer just a small amount of cream cheese on their bagel, referring to this by its Yiddish name, a "schmear." The problem is, bagels have become so popular that fakes are now common. The fakes are simply baked, or, more commonly, steamed and then baked. These forgeries can be detected by examining the bottom of the bagel; if there's a bumpy grid pattern, you've been duped! Steamed bagels are more like bread rolls, with none of the character of a real bagel.

Some say that the best bagels in town are to be found at the two **Ess-A-Bagel** locations (831 Third Avenue, 980-1010; 359 First Avenue, 260-2252), famous for producing outsize bagels that old folks complain are too damn big. The best combo, as far as I'm concerned, is their cinnamon-raisin bagel with just a schmear of vegetable cream cheese, but it's hard to get them to give you just a schmear — they insist on loading the bagel with cream cheese. Also popular is **Columbia Bagels** (2836 Broadway, 222-3200), making a product so good that they named the neighborhood university after this humble shop. **H & H** (2239 Broadway, 595-8003) is another Upper West Side favorite, pretentiously calling theirs "the official bagel of New York." As far as I'm concerned, though, careless franchising has substantially weakened their product. My greatest praise is reserved for a tiny shoebox of a place on the Lower East Side that tends to overboil its normal-sized bagels so that the crust is a little more unyielding than usual and the interior somewhat denser and chewier: **Motty's Bagels** (39 Essex Street, 260-4786).

Most bagel stores will also sell you the lox, sable, and other smoked and cured fish that, with cream cheese, are the most prized bagel toppings. Since they're sold to a captive audience, these accompaniments are sometimes not of the highest quality or as fresh as they might be. If you become a true fanatic, you'll have to go elsewhere to get your fish, like the hallowed **Russ & Daughters** (179 East Houston Street, 475-4880) on the Lower East Side or **Barney Greengrass** ("the Sturgeon King" — 541 Amsterdam Avenue, 724-4707) on the Upper West Side.

For a fascinating alternative to bagels, try bialys, the onion-filled disks originating in Bialystok, Poland. Most bagel stores sell them, but they're vastly inferior to the ones made at **Kossar's** (367 Grand Street, 473-4810), Manhattan's only remaining bialy bakery, where they have always made a garlic version in addition to the regulation onion. Bialys are more perishable than bagels — they must be eaten immediately or else toasted and scarfed within 12 hours, otherwise you might as well be eating a piece of cardboard. The poppy-seed-dotted long rolls call bulkas are more durable, and double surprisingly well for baguettes when you're making sandwiches.

SECRET
BARBECUE

❧

Admittedly, New York's not a barbecue town — like Kansas City, Memphis, or Lockhart, Texas — but based on the premise that food from anywhere in the world can be found here if you dig hard enough, you can bet there's some great 'cue in the metropolis. Forget about the most visible places, like Tennessee Mountain, the Hog Pit, and Brother's Barbecue — tourist traps all, with a pallid, under-smoked product. Here are three places that do it right, in descending order of preference.

Make a pilgrimage to **Mississippi Bar-B-Que** (201–05 Murdock Avenue, Ozone Park, Queens, 718-776-3446) and the neighborhood itself will make you feel like you're in the Deep South — for about five minutes, until a plane from nearby Kennedy Airport swooshes overhead. Ribs are the things to grab, and don't forget the soul-food sides and the heavenly banana pudding.

Manhattan barbecues are at a disadvantage since municipal laws prohibit a smoking operation that's very smoky. Nevertheless, cunning proprietors have found ways to overcome this problem. At **Virgil's Real Barbecue** (152 West 44th Street, 921-9494), they let plenty of wood smoke seep into the room, so you'll taste plenty of it when you chow down on the meat. Skip the beef and chicken in favor of the pork ribs or the lamb, and dig the incredible biscuits that come gratis with the meal.

Finally, there's **Duke's** (99 East 19th Street, 260-2922), conveniently located in the Flatiron District and offering acceptable brisket and chicken, with many sandwiches available and a pleasant-enough roadhouse atmosphere. Folks also praise the dry-rubbed ribs and collard greens.

SECRET

BARS

❊

When I first came to New York from Wisconsin, bars were on the wane. Of course, there were hotel bars where business people lingered — bored out of their minds — and seedy dives with grimy neon signs where old men sat glued to their seats and nursed Buds. Lots of things have happened since then: there's been a beer revolution that's attracted new patrons to brew pubs (see Secret Brew Pubs) in search of exotic suds; ditto for single-malt scotches, ports, wines, and even gold-label tequilas. Given the escalating ticket prices for many forms of entertainment, a night of drinking seems like a cheap alternative. It would take a whole book to dissect the bar scene, but here's a thumbnail sketch of the types of establishments that make up the alcoholic smorgasbord.

Like Tokyo's Ginza, Greenwich Village and the Lower East Side abound in theme bars, and East 14th Street has a couple of the greatest. **Barmacy** (538 East 14th Street, 228-2240) purloined its fixtures from an old apothecary, including nifty two-person booths, old greeting cards, well-thumbed paperbacks, and glass showcases crammed with forgotten products: Mufti Shoe White, Prophylactic

Tooth Powder, trusses, witch hazel, and something called Aniskin, uses unknown. A couple of blocks west is **Beauty Bar** (231 East 14th Street, 539-1389), where you can enjoy a drink under one of those massive streamlined hair dryers. If you wish you were in California instead of New York, check out **Lucy's Retired Surfers** (530 Columbus Avenue, 787-3009), where the decor runs to Day-Glo surfboards and the crowd quaffs beach-themed cocktails. **Küsh** (183 Orchard Street, 677-7328) recreates a Moroccan village with its decor.

Or go really retro by visiting the city's oldest bars, like **McSorley's** (15 East 7th Street, 473-9148), which has been around since Lincoln's time and has the stuff on the walls to prove it, or **Fraunces Tavern** (54 Pearl Street, 269-0144), where a weeping George Washington said farewell to his troops in 1783. For a little literary history, hoist one at the **White Horse Tavern** (567 Hudson Street, 989-3956), where Dylan Thomas drank himself to death, or the **Cedar Tavern** (82 University Place, 929-9089), beloved of the beats and the abstract expressionists. Or try the bar at the **Algonquin Hotel** (59 West 44th Street, 840-6800), made famous by Dorothy Parker and her roundtable in the '20s and still host to visiting literary celebs.

The true beer worshiper will dock at **d.b.a.** (41 First Avenue, 475-5097), which boasts 14 taps and 80 bottled beers in addition to a fine selection of single-malt scotches and top-shelf tequilas. An establishment in the West Village with similar pretensions is **Blind Tiger Ale House** (518 Hudson Street, 675-3848), which also excels at small-batch bourbons. Of course, the true beer perfectionist won't be satisfied with anything but his or her own. In which case, that person should visit **Little Shop of Hops** (9 East 37th Street, 685-8334), which carries all manner of home-brewing equipment.

A few other recommendations: the comfy, wood-paneled **King Cole Bar** at the St. Regis Hotel (Fifth Avenue and 55th Street, 753-4500) sports a Maxfield Parrish mural dating from 1906; **Puffy's Tavern** (81 Hudson Street, 766-9159) is a Tribeca dive preferred by artists who were there before the neighborhood was invaded by wealthy loft-dwellers; **Bubble Lounge** (228 West Broadway, 431-3433) is a chic-er Tribeca spot that specializes in champagne and purveys a few modest snacks; **Russian Vodka Room** (265 West 52nd Street, 307-5835) is just what its name says and no more; **Shark Bar** (307 Amsterdam Avenue, 874-8500) is a popular Upper West Side watering hole with a soul-food menu.

SECRET

BATH

❧

Who doesn't like to be pampered at bathtime? Or is unwilling to pay a little more for French milled soap shot with rosemary, moisturizing bath salts instead of Mister Bubble, or even a cadre of rubber ducks to be floated in the privacy of one's own tub? Bath obsession qualifies as one of the major trends of the late '90s, and Gotham has no lack of shops specializing in luxury bath needs.

My favorite is **Savon** (35 Christopher Street, 463-SOAP) a Village store that crams an inordinate number of toiletries into a tiny space. On a recent visit I spotted an intriguing array of products: cinnamon room fragrance, inflatable bath pillows, natural sponges, evening-primrose bath oil, Monkey-brand black tooth powder, sea-herb foaming bath, and little ceramic soap dishes shaped like Victorian footed tubs. **Fragrance Shoppe** (21 East 7th Street, 254-8950) in

the East Village not only carries similar products, but also custom blends bath oils and body washes, as does **Bath Island** (469 Amsterdam Avenue, 787-9415), which boasts nearly 100 scent combinations in their range of custom-formulated products.

Origins (402 West Broadway, 219-9764), located on a busy Soho corner, does an organic take on bath products and also features aromatherapy nostrums (see also Secret Aromatherapy).

SECRET

BATHROOMS

It's a bathroom-challenged city, and attempts to increase the number of public restrooms have bogged down in recent years over petty political issues. Even our quality-of-life-oriented mayor has been unable to improve the situation, though he'll see you thrown in prison overnight if he catches you peeing in an unauthorized spot — like behind a dumpster. So, if you decide to go al fresco, you've got to be canny about choosing a place.

Here are some alternatives: Every major department store has washrooms, like Macy's, Bloomingdales, and Lord & Taylor, although they hide them and you'll probably have to ask a clerk for directions. Parks like Union Square, Tompkins Square, Central Park, East River Park, Riverside Park, Washington Square, and Abingdon Square still have public restrooms dating from a much earlier age, though they are not in pristine condition. In an emergency, you can walk into almost any bar, act like you're going to get a drink, and then seek out the wc. Ditto most of the city's fast-food franchises. Even though McDonald's will usually not have a visible restroom, if you ask at the counter the employees will buzz you in through an unmarked door.

My best advice, though, is to drop in at Starbucks, which has 55 locations (at last count) in Manhattan alone. The key usually sits on a counter near the rear of the coffee emporium, and any patron, real or fictitious, can grab it and let himself or herself into the bathroom.

If you are really obsessed with knowing where all the public restrooms are, buy a copy of the book *Where to Go in New York*, which is available in the New York section of many Barnes & Noble bookstores. And, by the way, all the B & N superstores have public restrooms, too.

SECRET
BEAST
⚜

On one hand, there are the excursion boats that circumnavigate the island like the **Circle Line** (Pier 83 at 42nd Street and the Hudson River, 563-2000), and the ferries that connect Manhattan with Jersey, Staten Island, and Queens, all offering relaxing views of the Statue of Liberty and other bay and Hudson River landmarks; on the other hand, there's the **Beast** (Pier 16, South Street Seaport, 630-8888). This 69-foot speedboat, painted to look like a psychedelic shark, churns up the waters around lower Manhattan during a half-hour thrill ride at speeds that top out at 45 mph. For folks with deep pockets (adults $15, children $10) and a taste for the bizarre, the Beast delivers.

S E C R E T

BED-AND-BREAKFAST

✢

When my mother-in-law comes to town, I don't put her up in an impersonal midtown hotel — she snoozes at a bed-and-breakfast a few blocks from my apartment. At a fraction of the cost of most hotels she gets a pleasant — but not large — room in a handsome brownstone with a window overlooking a shady street.

In a city that never seems to have enough hotel rooms, bed-and-breakfasts fill a niche for budget-conscious travelers who prefer to stay in residential neighborhoods rather than tourist-clogged zones. And while rural bed-and-breakfasts can be creepy, with the eccentric landlady in your face all the time, at many city establishments you'll never even meet your host. This is because the real-estate situation in the city is so tight that nobody ever gives up an apartment, even if the owner or lessee moves out of town or shacks up with somebody who has their own apartment. The idea eventually occurs to these absentee tenants that their empty apartments can be turned into cash cows. (Add it up: if you pay $600 a month for a cute little studio in Chelsea and charge $85 per night by just putting a quart of orange juice in the refrigerator and buying a dozen donuts, your profits will build to a substantial sum.)

A large proportion of these bed-and-breakfasts are operated semi-legally, so the networks that book them rarely advertise. Look in the business pages at the rear of the residential phone book, though, and you'll see tons of listings, generally located in the part of town where the accommodations are offered: **Bed & Breakfast** (150 West End Avenue, 874-4308), **Bed & Breakfast A New World** (150 Fifth Avenue, 675-5600), **Bed & Breakfast Accommodations**

(520 East 76th Street, 472-2000), and, my favorite, **Bed & Breakfast Network of New York** (130 Barrow Street, 645-8134).

S E C R E T
BIKING
⚜

Getting around by cab or bus can be a pain in the ass on account of the heavy traffic in many parts of town. An ideal way to circumvent this and see a good deal of the city in the process is to rent a bike. You think I'm crazy, right? Naturally, it's not like riding in the suburbs, where you can cruise down tranquil streets with your mind on autopilot. In town, you must attain a Zen-like state of concentration as you zoom in and out of traffic and cruise illegally through red lights with one eye out for coppers.

But if the busy streets are not for you, there are plenty of quiet thoroughfares as well. **Central Park** has some of the city's best bike trails, although they're crowded at peak times with joggers and skaters as well as bicyclists. Better are some of the paths that run along the rivers. Enter the **East River Park** by the bridges that span Franklin D. Roosevelt Drive at 10th, 6th, or Houston Streets; the **Hudson River Promenade** at Chambers, Christopher, or 23rd Streets; or **Riverside Park** (Hudson River) at 72nd, 79th, or 90th Streets. Bikes are also permitted on the subways, although you may be prevented from entering subway cars during rush hours due to overcrowding. There is excellent biking at the Bronx's **Van Cortlandt Park** (last stop on the 1 or 9 trains) and Brooklyn's **Prospect Park** (best stops: 15th Street on the F or Prospect Park on the D).

But the mother of all great bike rides involves taking the ferry to **Staten Island**. Amazingly, the ferry is free, and it furnishes spectacular views of the upper harbor, Statue of Liberty, and lower-Manhattan skyline as you churn towards distant St. George. Queue up at the head of the line of the cars and you'll be admitted onto the automobile level of the ferry either before or after the cars have been loaded — riding with the cars at water level is one of the great pleasures of taking a bike. When you arrive, you'll have a choice of many excellent destinations: one of the best is **Clove Lakes Park**, almost the highest elevation on the island. Approach it by going west on Richmond Terrace along the waterfront, then turn inland at Clove Road, which skirts the park on its southern side. At the easternmost corner of the park this road intersects with Victory Boulevard, which takes you back to the ferry terminal via Bay Street, and it's a hair-raising downhill ride all the way! The entire circuit is about eight miles.

Indispensable for any bike trip in the metropolis is the *Hagstrom New York City 5 Borough Atlas* (see Secret Maps). The affiliated **Metro Bicycle Stores** rent mountain bikes or 10-speeds, with a compulsory helmet, for $6 per hour or $25 per day. They're conveniently located in several Manhattan neighborhoods: Midtown (340 West 47th Street, 581-4500), Upper East Side (1311 Lexington Avenue, 427-4450), Upper West Side (321 West 96th Street, 663-7531), East Village (332 East 14th Street, 228-4344), Chelsea (546 Avenue of the Americas, 255-5100), and Soho (417 Canal Street, 334-8000). Or if you intend to rent for several days, maybe even the entire duration of your visit, consider buying a used bike at a flea market (see Secret Flea Markets and Secret Markets), where a vintage three-speed in decent condition can often be had for $75 or so. Abandon it when you depart, or sell it back to the flea-market vendor.

BIRDS OF PREY
❖

New York is a birdwatcher's paradise. I know that sounds ridiculous, but the city possesses wetlands in abundance, like **Jamaica Bay Wildlife Refuge**, where hundreds of waterfowl may be observed during a pleasant and well-marked marsh hike. (To get there, leave the A train at the Broad Channel stop, then walk East on 8th Road four blocks and north on Cross Bay Boulevard about three-quarters of a mile.)

Songbirds, too, may be observed in profusion, especially in parkland like **Central Park** and **Inwood Hill**. For neophytes, or those who like to hang with other birdwatchers, **Urban Park Rangers** (1-888-NYPARKS) offers free birding expeditions in city parks in all five boroughs. Because the city is on the migratory paths of many species, birdwatching in the autumn is particularly rich.

But among the plethora of winged creatures found in the city, the most surprising group is the birds of prey, which seem totally out of place in the metropolis. They're attracted by the aforementioned songbirds, and, even more important, by vermin — the mice and rats that make such nice snacks. Plump pigeons, too, are sitting ducks for all sorts of urban raptors: red-tailed hawks, turkey vultures, kestrels, and peregrine falcons, some of whom nest in the wooden water towers that grace New York's high-rise apartment buildings. The **Audubon Society** (71 West 23rd Street, 691-7483) offers programs that usually include two lectures and two birdwatching expeditions, emphasizing raptors and other urban birds. Less formal is the society's Hawkwatch program (360-2774), conducted at Central Park's Belvedere Castle. It runs from mid-August to mid-December,

11 A.M. to 4 P.M. every day, often providing you with the opportunity
to see hundreds of raptors wheeling around the park at one time.

S E C R E T
BLUES
❖

The Big Apple isn't a blues town like Memphis or Chicago, but we
tread water with a couple of decent, every-night blues venues:
Chicago Blues (73 Eighth Avenue, 924-9755) in the Village; and
Manny's Car Wash (1558 Third Avenue, 369-2583), a rare Upper
East Side music venue, with no cover charge on Sunday and Monday
evenings. Big-name blues acts sometimes showcase for record exec-
utives and their pals at **Tramps** and the **Bottom Line** (see Secret
Rock Clubs).

S E C R E T
BOARDWALKS
❖

Since the late nineteenth century, boardwalks have been a main
feature of America's East Coast seascape, and the merest glimpse of
one is enough to induce nostalgia for warm afternoons spent drows-
ing lazily on the beach. Just listen to the Coasters' song "Under the
Boardwalk": the inspiration was the **Riegelmann Boardwalk**,
which runs for four miles along Brooklyn's barrier island, now silted
to the mainland, through Sea Gate, Coney Island, and Brighton

Beach. In doing so, it passes enough attractions to make a hike of the entire length worthwhile.

Any of the Coney Island subway lines (B, D, F, and N) will deposit you at Stillwell Avenue in a rococo station made to handle summer crowds via a series of tilting and staired shunts. The broken-down station shops are evocative of beach expeditions of 60 years ago, but don't let their seedy quality prevent you from enjoying the homemade fudge, saltwater taffy, and caramel apples. Of course, you won't be able to resist the hot dogs at Nathan's as you make your way to the boardwalk (see Secret Hot Dogs). Other attractions on Surf Avenue, the area's commercial hub, include flea markets, ice-cream parlors, a bumper-car ride, and the **Coney Island Museum** (1208 Surf Avenue, 718-372-5159, Web site: coneyisland.brooklyn. ny.us/framesite/indexwindow.html), the successor to a popular counterculture boardwalk freakshow called Sideshows by the Sea-shore that included a bearded lady, a sword swallower, and a tattooed man.

Landmarks along this end of the boardwalk: the **Cyclone**, the city's last real roller coaster (see Secret Roller Coaster); **Wonder Wheel**, the world's tallest Ferris wheel, with two concentric rings of cars that swing breathtakingly back and forth as the wheel turns; and the notorious parachute jump, moved here from the 1939 World's Fair and inoperable since the '60s. Also take a walk through some of the byways north of the boardwalk, which harbor decaying carnie attractions, games of chance, go-kart tracks, and small-scale thrill rides, fascinating even in the off-season months.

Proceeding east along the boardwalk, you'll be dazzled by the vast sweep of the ocean broken only by the land masses of the Rock-aways further east and the Jersey Shore to the west. The sheer volume of ocean traffic — barges, cargo steamers, sailboats, and party-fishing boats puttering back to Sheepshead Bay (see Secret Fishing) — is impressive. On the eastern verge of Coney Island is the **New York Aquarium** (718-265-3474), where the specimens, including beluga whales, sharks, and penguins, are much more interesting than the architecture. Kids dig the hands-on exhibit of horseshoe crabs.

As you stroll further east on the boardwalk, a strange transformation takes place. The crowd stops speaking English and Spanish and picks up Russian. You're entering Brighton Beach, known colloquially as "Little Odessa" (see Secret Russian), where the boardwalk comes alive on summer evenings with buskers playing accordions, violins, and guitars and singing plaintive melodies. There is also a string of boardwalk cafés serving Russian food at reasonable prices. For beachgoers, this stretch of sand is less crowded in summer months.

Other boardwalks in the city include a really secret crescent-shaped one at **Manhattan Beach** on the far-eastern end of Coney Island, a private-seeming public beach that's difficult to get to by public transportation. (Hint: It's a walk of about a mile from the Sheepshead Bay stop on the D and Q trains and you'll need a Hagstrom map [see Secret Maps].) There's another in the Bronx at **Orchard Beach** in Pelham Bay Park, attainable by bus from the last stop on the 6 train. Once again, you'll need a map, but at both of these less-visited boardwalks you'll have the chance to meet groups of New Yorkers that you won't see in more touristy spots.

SECRET

BOTANICAL
GARDENS

❦

Two major botanical gardens vie for your attention. The larger of the two, located in the Bronx, declares its superiority by calling itself the **New York Botanical Garden** (200th Street and Southern Boulevard, 718-817-8700). The 250-acre site includes a glass-domed conservatory in the Victorian style, many far-flung flower beds, a gift shop with New Age overtones, a miniforest, a snuff mill (in the late eighteenth century this land was the estate of the tobacco-growing Lorillard family), and a rather dull composting exhibition among its 44 listed attractions. Don't fall for their trick of making you cough up $10 to sample them all; instead spring for the modest $3 ticket. But do pay an additional $1 for the tram, a miniature two-car train that gives you a 20-minute introduction to the park and lets you disembark once and get on again — it will save on shoe leather. The best part is the forest trail, which overlooks a decent-sized waterfall on the Bronx River. Although it's forbidden, some of the best hiking is off the marked trails. You can go beyond the barrier, for example, at the waterfall overlook and find a delightful sun-dappled path that leads into the thickest part of the woods and delivers unexpected river views (and river access). Don't tell them I told you. No one will see you because all the employees of the garden are busy selling stuff.

Which explains why I like the **Brooklyn Botanic Garden** (Eastern Parkway and Washington Avenue, 718-622-4433), even though it is a fraction of the size. There's a beautiful Japanese pond with lilies, cherry blossoms, ducks, and a pagoda. It's especially nice in the wintertime, when you can look through holes in the ice and see foot-long goldfish swimming by sluggishly. The conservatory, consisting of several newly built, glassed-in environments, also rocks in the wintertime when a stroll through the desert is just the thing to dispel the blahs. On the western side of the botanical garden, which wraps around the Brooklyn Museum, an unparalleled rose garden blooms most of the summer. Best of all — due to its smaller area, this garden is more doable than its Bronx counterpart.

S E C R E T

BREW PUBS

⚜

A dozen or so brew pubs — bars that brew their own beer in relatively small batches — have opened in the last three years, and about half have already closed. The reason: the homemade beer usually stinks. But there are a couple of exceptions: **Heartland Brewery** (35 Union Square West, 645-3400; 1285 Sixth Avenue, 582-8244) taps five varieties of home brew on a rotating basis of which the lighter brews, like the wheat beer, are the best. It also serves some of the best bar food in town, including a righteous buffalo burger and a pu pu platter (appetizer assortment) of layered plates on a metal rack filled with chow from all over the world. **Times Square Brewery** (160 West 42nd Street, 398-1234) has some surprisingly good liquid products as well, and a decent German-inflected menu to match. The spectacular view of the Hudson River at **Chelsea Brewing** (Pier 62 at Chelsea Piers, enter at West 23rd Street, 336-6440) overshadows the good beer and eats.

SECRET

BROOKLYN BRIDGE

✤

When it opened in 1883, the **Brooklyn Bridge** was declared the Eighth Wonder of the World: the longest bridge in existence, it soared 1,595.5 feet from tower to tower and its massive suspension cables were made from 14,357 miles of wire. The bridge was designed by John Augustus Roebling, who died in 1867, before the project was even under construction. He was replaced by his son Washington, who, along with many other workers (several of whom died), contracted caisson disease as a result of working underwater in bottomless wooden boxes while excavating the footings of the bridge. This illness is now known as the bends, but the cause and remedy were unknown at the time. Washington was crippled by the disease, and had to supervise the final stages of construction from his nearby Brooklyn apartment, seated in a wheelchair and using binoculars.

The opening of the bridge was attended by huge crowds for whom the structure was an awe-inspiring and fear-provoking marvel (it still is). Someone yelled that the bridge was collapsing, and a stampede ensued in which 12 people were trampled to death. Nowadays, you can perambulate the bridge's wooden walkway between Manhattan and Brooklyn with complete confidence, and the view from the bridge is one of the city's greatest sights, with the Brooklyn Heights Promenade and the Navy Yard visible on the Brooklyn side, and the South Street Seaport and Lower East Side projects (high-rise apartment houses for the poor) on the Manhattan side. To get to the Manhattan side of the walkway, take the 6 train to the City Hall stop. For a guided tour of the bridge, see Secret Walking Tours.

Other bridges you can cross on foot include the **Williamsburg Bridge** over the East River and the **George Washington Bridge** over the Hudson.

SECRET

BURLESQUE

✣

When Mayor Giuliani closed the peep shows (see Secret Sex), the death knell of sexual entertainment didn't toll. The ancient art of burlesque was revived at a number of downtown locations, merging predictably with the performance art that's been an entertainment staple in the neighborhood for two decades. Actually, the sex element has always been there, as anyone who saw Karen Finley lewdly humping a statue of the Virgin Mary or shoving yams up her behind in the early '80s can testify.

Friday and Saturday evenings at midnight, the **Blue Angel Cabaret** happens at the **House of Candles** (99 Stanton Street, 591-2498, Web site: www.blueangel.com), successor to a Tribeca strip club, now closed, that emphasized sex-worker empowerment while featuring lap dances and nudie shows. The current program features barely clothed torch singers, sword swallowers, fire eaters, and a performer who recites poems while wearing a diaphanous sack and playing a flashlight over her body. **Red Vixen Burlesque** presents a similar mix at **Flamingo East** (219 Second Avenue, 533-2860) on Sunday nights, hosted by a raconteur in an ill-fitting double-breasted suit who tells dirty jokes, though the entertainment is strictly PG 13 as far as I'm concerned. There's also **Grindhouse Alternative Burlesque** on Tuesdays at **Tonic** (107 Norfolk Street, 358-7501). These acts are likely to migrate to other bars over the course of time, so check listings in Secret Periodicals for these and other burlesque events.

SECRET
CABARET

❧

The art of cabaret — small-scale entertainment in an intimate room, often involving just a singer and piano player doing show tunes — is alive and well in New York. Prime venues include **Don't Tell Mama** (343 West 46th Street, 757-0788) in the Theater District, and the even smaller **Eighty Eight's** (228 West 10th Street, 924-0088) down in the Village. Both have a cover charge of about $10 and a two-drink minimum, so an evening out will set you back $20 or so. There are also big-ticket rooms around town that feature name talent, like the indomitable **Café Carlyle** (35 East 76th Street, 570-7189) at the eponymous hotel; here, New York's favorite cabaret artiste, Bobby Short, often perches on the piano bench. The action will set you back at least $50, and dinner is available at a substantial extra charge. Follow the scene in the Cabaret section of *Time Out New York*.

S E C R E T

CDs

✦

The big chains — Tower, Sam Goody, and HMV — dominate the record-selling business in New York, and each features huge boxes of big-label releases just inside its front door so you don't have to bother going inside and looking around for more obscure recordings. If you're in a subversive mood, however, or want to find something that's not simplistic rock or rap, you've got to be a little more circumspect in your shopping habits.

Other Music (15 East 4th Street, 477-8150) is provocatively poised directly opposite Tower Records, and specializes in small-label and local music, mainly rock, experimental, and ambient. For an indie record store, prices are amazingly low. Another joint with a good selection in a similar vein is **Mondo Kim's** (6 St. Marks Place, 598-9915), a four-story record palace located on a strip in the East Village tenderloin that's home to several record stores, including some, like **Sounds** (16 Saint Marks Place, 677-2727), that specialize in used recordings. One of my favorite establishments, walking the tightrope between indie and major-label, is unexpectedly located in Soho: **Rock's in Your Hear** (157 Prince Street, 475-6729).

Discount is a word you might not normally associate with New York, but the two **Disc-O-Rama** stores (40 Union Square West, 260-8616; 186 West 4th Street, 206-8417) sell new-release CDs for the astonishing price of $9.99 — and I challenge you to better that anywhere in the country. **Record Explosion** (507 Fifth Avenue, 661-6642; 176 Broadway, 693-1510) remainders lots of classical and opera CDs and records, as does the **Tower Records Clearance Outlet** (20 East 4th Street, 228-7317). Probably the best store for jazz, only slightly discounted, is **J & R Music World** (23 Park Row, 238-9000), just across the street from City Hall.

More interesting are the stores that cater to disc jockeys and specialize in limited-edition vinyl as well as CD releases reflecting all the latest dance styles — like rave, ambient, trance, house, acid jazz, trip hop, and other styles too new to have names (that I know of, that is). They're mainly located in the West and East Villages, I'm not sure why, and include **Vinylmania** (60 Carmine Street, 924-7723), **Sonic Groove** (41 Carmine Street, 675-5284), and **Rebel Rebel** (319 Bleecker Street, 989-0770), which specializes in British CDs. **Throb** (211 East 14th Street, 533-2328) also carries cool DJ paraphernalia — like heavy-duty record cases in psychedelic patterns and T-shirts — in addition to the latest dance tracks. Among the stores specializing in techno, rave, and related styles are **Adult Crash** (66 Avenue A, 387-0558) and **Strange** (445 East 9th Street, 505-3025).

Some collectors still refuse to buy CDs, concentrating on oldies in out-of-print vinyl. Those interested in new wave and punk throng to **Bleecker Bob's** (118 West 3rd Street, 477-7902). Those interested in older rock styles go to **House of Oldies** (35 Carmine Street, 243-0500).

The most spectacular record store in town is undoubtedly the new **Virgin Records** store at Times Square (1790 Broadway, 1-800-491-8787). It's built on multiple levels receding into the concrete substratum of the square, and features multiple DJs spinning a surprisingly international selection of stuff in addition to a rather repulsive Virgin Records clothing boutique. Underneath it all is a bookstore and then a multiplex cinema — keep descending and you'll feel like you're almost all the way to China, or maybe in the merchandising equivalent of hell.

Another subterranean retailer is the **nameless record store** one flight above the N and R platform at the Times Square subway station (840-0580), which has a soberingly large collection of most of the Latin styles from the Caribbean and South America. It's the only thing that would keep me in that hideous station.

SECRET
CHARMING ENCLAVES

Manhattan's 71,000 dwellings are mainly tenements, high-rise apartments, and single-family townhouses, the latter often broken up into apartments. But occasionally this predictable grid falters, and the oddities produced by these lapses make for some enjoyable viewing.

Pomander Walk is a double row of storybook Tudor cottages on a pedestrian lane that runs from West 94th to West 95th Street just east of West End Avenue. Built in 1922, they were a re-creation of the stage set for an English play of the same name that was a hit on Broadway in 1911. You won't be able to walk among the cottages unless you know someone who lives there, but the view through the wrought-iron fence is one of the city's oddest.

Ditto **Sniffen Court**, an urban enclave of 10 ornate Romanesque Revival carriage houses built in the 1850s and converted to residential use. Located just off East 36th Street between Lexington and Third Avenues, the two-story stables flank a paved courtyard decorated with iron horse heads. A similar cul de sac is found just off 10 Grove Street in the West Village. Known today as **Grove Court**, this irregular row of brick-faced workingmen's cottages,

visible through an iron fence, was built in 1854 and was first known as Mixed Ale Alley.

One mews — the British term for a row of stables with residences above — that you can actually walk on is **Washington Mews**, located just above Washington Square, now part of New York University. Between Fifth Avenue and University Place, it consists of a row of nineteenth-century stables on the north side. The stucco houses on the south side date back to 1939, and a walk through this courtyard paved with Belgian blocks will give you a sense of being somewhere other than New York City.

SECRET

CHEAP HOTELS

✢

To anyone coming from anywhere else in the world (with the possible exceptions of Tokyo, Hong Kong, and Los Angeles), New York's hotels are shockingly priced. A modest room near Rockefeller Center or Times Square can often run $300 or more, and, unlike Paris, there is no elaborate network of small and acceptable neighborhood two-star establishments to fall back on. Many tourists solve this problem by buying tour packages that include hotel, or by booking a room in a chain motel in the backwoods of New Jersey or Westchester, or near one of the airports. This entails commutes of at least an hour each way to get to the sights, leaving you exhausted and dampening your desire to stay late in town to sample the nightlife.

But if you scan the city's hotelscape you'll see a few bargains, especially if you're willing to book early. As a bonus, many of these places are located in residential neighborhoods far from the noise and turmoil of the tourist destinations, giving you the sensation of actually living in the city. **Westpark Hotel** (308 West 58th Street, 246-6440, single $95, double $110) is located steps away from Lincoln Center and Central Park at the gateway to the Upper West Side. Furnishings are spartan and rooms are small, but you won't be spending much time there anyway. For a little more luxury in the same neighborhood, try the **Mayflower** (15 Central Park West, 265-0060, single $165, double $180), which is situated right on the park and offers larger rooms and a bar and restaurant on the premises. A room with a view of the park will cost you more. Another Upper West Side bargain is the **Hotel Beacon** (2130 Broadway, 787-1100, single $135, double $155), where the value of each room is enhanced by a kitchenette, allowing you to economize on meals and make use of the bounty found at the city's many farmers' markets.

But most of the legendary and economical small hotels are downtown. The **Gramercy Park Hotel** (2 Lexington Avenue, 475-4320, single $145, double $160), where area college students park their parents, is adjacent to the city's premier private park, and the doorman has a key that admits hotel guests so they can promenade with the rich people whose residences ring the park. The **Herald Square** (19 West 31st Street, 279-4017, single $95, double $105) is in a mercantile neighborhood not far from Macy's and offers basic rooms kept spotlessly clean. Farther afield, but in the same general area, is the **Arlington Hotel** (18 West 25th Street, 645-3990, single or double $95), recommended by the photographer who worked on this book, and the even cheaper **Senton Hotel** (39 West 27th Street, single $50, double $60), which has recently been refurbished. My favorite hotel bargain is in the midst of the Village: the **Washington Square Hotel** (103 Waverly Place, 777-9515, single $110, double

$129), deliriously close to all forms of transportation and pleasantly situated on a tree-lined street just off the square.

Cheaper accommodations are also available within the surprisingly large network of bed-and-breakfasts (see Secret Bed-and-Breakfast), but for rock-bottom prices you can't beat the youth-hostel system. New York's premiere establishment, **Hosteling International New York** (891 Amsterdam Avenue, 932-2300, around $30 per night), has 480 beds set out in a variety of dormitory-style configurations. It's located in a landmark building in a pleasant, working-class section of the Upper West Side. On a recent visit I found many of the residents occupying tables on a street-side terrace and happily chatting. Other hostels in town include Harlem's **International House Sugar Hill** (722 St. Nicholas Avenue, 926-7030), **Banana Bungalow** (250 West 77th Street, 769-2441) on the Upper West Side, and the **Gershwin Hotel** (7 East 27th Street, 545-8000), a combination hotel and hostel near Madison Square Park, where dorm-style rooms run $22, with hotel accommodations as low as $75.

SECRET

CHELSEA GALLERIES

✤

The Chelsea section of Manhattan's far-west side has long since displaced Soho as the home of avant-garde art contriving to become mainstream. This former warehouse district hosts galleries far larger and grander than their Soho counterparts, making for more shows of large paintings and sculpture, and gallery walking in this region is still a relatively relaxing experience, especially if you can go on weekdays. American up-and-comers like Nan Goldin, John Ahearn, Lynda Benglis, and Fang Lijun cut their eyeteeth here, as well as prominent artists from foreign countries, especially the British Isles. And if you see an opening in progress in the early evening – with patrons spilling out into the street, cocktails in hand – chances are you can merge with the crowd and join in the fun without being identified as an interloper.

Hot exhibition spots include **Max Protech** (511 West 22nd Street, 633-6999), **Paula Cooper** (534 West 21st Street, 255-1105), **Cheim and Reid** (521 West 23rd Street, 242-7727), and **Hearn** (530 West 22nd Street, 727-7366), but for a choice selection of current shows consult the *New Yorker*'s "Goings On about Town," which includes a section headed "Galleries — Chelsea."

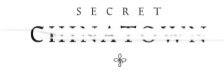

SECRET
CHINATOWN

✿

Pass a succession of shrines — each anchored by a statue of Buddha wafting incense and stacked with oranges — to arrive at a two-story Buddha mired in red carpet and strung with tiny lights. We're in the **Mahayana Temple** (133 Canal Street, 925-8787), whose yellow facade is guarded by golden dogs who glare impassively as brown-cloaked monks drift in and out. Visitors are welcome, as long as they observe the posted imprecation: "Decent Clothes Is Required in the Buddhist Temple."

Thirty years ago, the five streets just south of Canal (Mott, Mulberry, Bayard, Baxter, and Doyers) formed Manhattan's Chinatown.

Now, in response to huge influxes of capital from Hong Kong and a relaxation of racist American immigration policies, Chinatown extends as far north as Delancey and as far east as Essex, comprising 10 times the area it did decades ago. The older streets of Chinatown are still worth visiting, dotted with curio shops and tourist-oriented restaurants, especially Doyers Street, a narrow alley that preserves an early-twentieth-century feel.

But just around the corner from the Mahayana Temple, running from Canal to Grand on Bowery, is Little Vietnam, one of the many minineighborhoods that now make up Greater Chinatown. At 85 Bowery is **Banh Mi So 1**, the city's best-known purveyor of Vietnamese sandwiches, delicious baguettes filled with barbecued pork, pâté, and pickled vegetables — France meets Southeast Asia. Right next door at 81 is a Vietnamese supermarket worth exploring, **Tan Ai Hoa**. One of my favorite restaurants is **Pho Tu Do** (119 Bowery, 966-2666), where the specialty is pho, cilantro-laced soups featuring rice noodles and thin-sliced raw beef that's dropped in at the last minute so it cooks as it arrives at the table.

At the north end of Little Vietnam is Grand Street, which is now the main drag of modern, working-class Chinatown. At nearby 91 Bowery is the **Music Palace** (925-4971), an ancient Bowery theater that is the last remaining movie house in Chinatown. Hong Kong productions are showcased and all the features are subtitled in English. A recent double bill included *Extreme Crisis*, a martial-arts film, and *Tricky King*, a comedy.

The intersection of Grand and Mott is Chinatown's greatest market district. Here fish vendors and greengrocers sell a breathtaking range of Asian products. At one fishmonger, I counted nine varieties of shrimp and 27 types of fresh fish. The fruit markets sell fresh lichee, pomegranate, and durian, a spiny, football-shaped fruit with a

creamy sweet flesh that smells like vomit. In this district, the best Chinese restaurant is **219 Grand Street Gourmet** (226-4231), where the specialty is baby pig over rice. Anything offered in the window is cheap; the evening menu is surprisingly expensive. A good choice in this region at any hour is **Bunga Raya** (157 Mott Street, 219-3688), a Malaysian restaurant that mixes Chinese, Indian, and aboriginal Malaysian flavors to produce dishes sold at stunningly low prices. Try roti canai, a coconut-laced curry served with a buttery flatbread.

Another main axis of Greater Chinatown is East Broadway, a formerly Jewish neighborhood that's been gradually overtaken. A great place for a dim-sum lunch is the glitzy **Triple Eight Palace** (88 East Broadway, 941-8886), one of the huge Hong Kong-style restaurants that have become a Chinatown signature. The dumplings and little snacks are pushed around the sprawling room on carts that pass every table, allowing you to examine and purchase small plates whenever you feel like it. There are dozens of offerings, including chicken feet, pork ribs with black-bean sauce, steamed pork buns, and shrimp dumplings. At the seafood station you can select wonderful mussels, clams, and tempura shrimp in a variety of savory sauces. Reflecting the Chinese passion for gambling, a neon-lit booth sells lottery tickets. The restaurant is approached via an escalator from the shopping mall at street level.

For a quieter corner of Chinatown, seek out Elizabeth Street. The **Elizabeth Center** (15 Elizabeth Street) is a bi-level mall with cosmetic and drug stalls on the main floor. All the action, however, is in the basement, where a number of vendors sell merchandise that kids love, including Japanese action figures, video games, key chains with cartoon characters, and other collectibles. It's worth a visit, whatever age you happen to be. Down the street is KCC

International Trading Corp., which specializes in Hello Kitty merchandise, featuring Kitty's demonic pals Badz Maru ("bad hair day" in Japanese), Pekkle the penguin, and newcomer Doraemon, "a cat-like robot from the 22nd century that takes many fantastic tools out of its fourth dimension pouch." Around the corner, don't miss **Chinatown Ice Cream Factory** (see Secret Ice Cream).

Much of Manhattan's Chinatown is on the tourist track. Instead explore the far reaches, like the highly recommended **Natural Restaurant** (88 Allen Street, 966-1325), where the specialties include conch, baby octopus, and ostrich at modest prices. Or consider trekking to one of New York's other Chinatowns. The biggest, rivaling Manhattan's in size, is Flushing, Queens. Just take the 7 train to the last stop and begin wandering along Main Street in either direction. There are two in Brooklyn: the oldest is on Sunset Park's Eighth Avenue, from 61st Street southward; the newest is centered on the Avenue U stop on the D train and moves along the avenue in both directions. Explore these areas as a lone tourist and you'll feel like an urban pioneer.

S E C R E T
CHOCOLATE
✤

With eight locations in Manhattan, Godiva Chocolatier has contrived to make its name synonymous with luxury chocolates. There's only one problem with that: its chocolates suck! To begin with, they have an oily quality that overshadows the chocolaty goodness. In addition, the fillings — mainly fruit-based — are runny and far too sweet. If you're trying to impress someone with your wealth, go Godiva, but if you really crave chocolate, look elsewhere.

Elsewhere for me is **Li-Lac Chocolates** (120 Christopher Street, 242-7374), an intimate shop that's like a time capsule; it first opened in 1923, and a succession of owners have kept it looking and tasting pretty much the same. The window is reason enough to visit, jammed with sculptures made of solid chocolate that change frequently according to holiday season and proprietors' whim. Sometimes it will be a midtown skyline, sometimes a Father's Day display of chocolate ties, cigars, and golf clubs. The dark chocolate is best, more coarsely textured than Godiva's, and not too sweet. Buy it in its most elemental form, as "break-up" — pure, amorphous chunks — or filled with nuts or soft caramel. Since all the chocolate is made in the back room, it can't get any fresher than this, and kids especially appreciate the store's collection of on-the-stick novelties, amazingly priced at 30¢ and up.

If you insist, I'll mention a few more places, none of which quite come up to Li-Lac. **Fifth Avenue Chocolatière** (506 Madison Avenue, 935-5454) has made its reputation by fabricating chocolate sculptures on demand, and is also famous for its caramels. For filled-chocolate assortments — like a Whitman's Sampler, only a million times better — check out **La Maison du Chocolat** (25 East 73rd Street, 744-7117), but remember that any place with a French name is going to be expensive. Truffle lovers flock to **Teuscher Chocolates** (25 East 61st Street, 751-8482), a Swiss firm that flies its wares in rather than manufacturing them on the premises. In Brooklyn, **JoMart Chocolates** (2917 Avenue R, 718-375-1277) turns out over 100 types of confection, including its signature "caranut" — coconut caramel smothered in chocolate.

S E C R E T
CINEMAS
❖

To outsiders, the movie ticket prices in town seem outlandishly high
— $8.75 or $9.00, depending on which first-run venue you choose.
Plus, there are no special deals like twilight or early-bird, and no
special coupon offers. At least the days are gone when the cinemas
were massed in just a few Midtown neighborhoods. Now you can
see a film in almost any part of town, although many of the new
multiplex cinemas are just as boxy and poorly designed as those in
the suburbs.

Many of the grand old cinemas have been demolished or multi-
plexed, leaving only a handful of houses with large auditoriums that
show just one feature at a time. Two that I recommend as thrilling
places to see a movie are the **Sony Astor Plaza** (Broadway and 44th
Street, 869-8340) and the **Cineplex Odeon Ziegfeld** (54th Street
just west of 6th Avenue, 505-CINE, #602). Both have huge screens,
great acoustics, and booming theater sound, and don't forget the
pleasure of hearing thousands of people laugh along with you.

There's one off-price multiplex in Manhattan, the wonderful **World-
wide** (54th Street between Eighth and Ninth Avenues, 505-CINE,
#610) — six theaters housed in a spectacular underground bunker.
Here you can see big features and art films about nine months after
their release for $3.

Speaking of art films, a couple of art houses persist in Midtown,
showing foreign-language films and small-budget indies: the **Paris
Theater** (58th Street west of Fifth Avenue, 688-3800) just across the
street from the Plaza Hotel, and the **Walter Reade Theater** (Lincoln
Center and West 65th Street, 336-5000), which specializes in series.

Downtown, of course, is where most of the indie action is. The most well-known of the theaters is the **Angelika Film Center** (Houston at Mercer Street, 777-FILM, #531). The Angelika has an exemplary snack bar, which serves sandwiches, coffees, and pastry treats, but, alas, the six screening rooms are small, uncomfortable, and marred by occasional subway noise. The **Quad** (13th Street between Fifth and Sixth Avenues, 255-8800) has even smaller theaters, but I find it charming anyway. The screening list favors gay and foreign films, and you can find a seat almost anytime. More serious cinephiles congregate at the **Film Forum** (209 West Houston Street, 727-8110), where memberships are available and showings are sometimes preceded by lectures. The three theaters have chair backs with miniature tags identifying celebrity donors. Even more serious is the **Anthology Film Archives** (Second Avenue and 2nd Street, 505-5110), located in a handsome old brick warehouse with a list of features including the foreign, the experimental, and the incredibly obscure.

Finally, there's the **Screening Room** (Corner of Varick and Canal Streets, 334-2100), which offers the novel combination of a film and a three-course gourmet meal for $30.

New York no longer has any drive-in movie theaters, but the next best thing is the **Bryant Park Summer Film Festival** (Sixth Avenue and 41st Street), where cinephiles enjoy a free movie every Monday evening during the summer beginning at sunset in the handsomely renovated park right behind the main branch of the New York Public Library. Bring a blanket and a sack supper.

SECRET

COFFEE

❧

The "city that never sleeps" would be snoozing 'round the clock if it weren't for coffee. The New Yorker unglues his or her eyes with a double latte early in the morning and doesn't stop drinking till the traditional late-dinner aperitif — a shot of espresso — is consumed. No wonder the metropolis always seems to be set on high speed.

A couple of years ago, the Seattle chain Starbucks attacked New York like an invading army, so that there are now over 50 in Manhattan alone (see Secret Bathrooms); frankly, their "overroasted" style of coffee tastes like office brew that sat on the warmer too long. Besides, at over $3 for some of the more elaborate concoctions, it's way too expensive. Seek out any of the Cuban lunch counters in town, among them **La Caridad** (2199 Broadway, 874-2780), **Havana Chelsea Luncheonette** (190 Eighth Avenue, 243-9421), and **Margon** (136 West 46th Street, 354-5013), for coffee with twice the flavor at less than half the price. If you want to sit down and relax with your cup, seek out one of the old-time Italian pastry shops, like **DeRobertis** (176 First Avenue, 674-7137) or **Caffe Dante** (81 MacDougal Street, 982-5275), where you'll still save money over Starbucks, or one of our homegrown coffee shops like **Grey Dog's Coffee** (33 Carmine Street, 462-0041), which also has great sandwiches and light meals. See also Secret Gay for more coffee bars where everyone is made welcome, queer or not.

My imprecation to avoid the big coffee-bar chains extends to whole beans as well. There are plenty of long-established beaneries in the city where you can enjoy the ambiance as well as an out-standing selection of beans and brewing contraptions. **Porto Rico**

Importing (201 Bleecker Street, 477-5421), whose name is Italian for "rich port," not a misspelling, offers an astounding array of coffee at discount prices. The king of the old-fashioned shops is **McNulty's** (109 Christopher Street, 242-5351), with 75 coffees and 35 loose teas ensconced in tip-out brass tubs, and a friendly, knowledgeable staff. Another good choice in a no-frills vein is **Empire Coffee & Tea** (592 Ninth Avenue, 586-1717), founded in 1908 and a relatively inexpensive source for top-shelf varieties like Tanzania Peaberry ($12.49 a pound), Jamaican Blue Mountain ($25 a pound), and Kona Hawaiian French Roast ($16 a pound). If you want to quaff like royalty, grab a permanent gold filter ($10.95) for your drip apparatus.

SECRET
CONTRACEPTION

❦

Condomania (351 Bleecker Street, 691-9442) seems to be very popular with tourists. As they stroll along the West Village's charming Bleecker Street, first they come to a full stop, then they point, then they giggle, then they step inside for more fun. Largely ignored by the locals, the store ostensibly specializes in prophylactics, but this merchandise, which is very serious business in a city that's the cradle of AIDS, was long ago eclipsed by sexual gag gifts, like the Pecker Stretcher (open the box to discover a tiny hospital stretcher) and a pair of huge boxer shorts with happy faces on it.

Another problem at Condomania is that the condoms are twice as expensive as everywhere else. Peek into the store, then buy elsewhere. Any of the big drug chains like **Duane Reade** or **Rite Aid** sell major-brand condoms at $7 or $8 per dozen, or discount brands for as little as $4. Displays are in plain sight, although usually at the back of the store. For other forms of sex-oriented merchandise, see Secret Sex and Secret Erotic Toys.

S E C R E T

COOKBOOKS

⚜

I'm prejudiced, but I think **Kitchen Arts & Letters** (1435 Lexington Avenue, 876-5550) is one of the greatest bookstores in the world. This double-wide storefront carries a bewildering array of food-related titles, from mainstream cookbooks, to food-science tomes, to memoirs, to out-of-print, to ethnic cookbooks, many from their native lands. A large proportion of the offerings are available no-where else in town. The kindly owner, Nahum Waxman, has created a friendly atmosphere for "foodies" (I hate that word) of every stripe, and the shop serves as a clearinghouse for information and contacts thanks to its knowledgeable staff members, who can find a way to obtain even the most obscure titles.

The library with the best collection of antiquarian cookbooks, dating back to Roman times, is, perversely, the **New York Academy of Medicine library** (1216 Fifth Avenue, 822-7200, Web site: www. nyam.org/library/about.html), which is open to the public on week-days. The 1929 bequest of Margaret Barclay Wilson, MD, this 10,000-item collection contains what is believed to be the earliest cookbook in the Western world — a ninth-century transcription of a work by Apicius that provides a surprising glimpse into the eating habits of the Romans.

SECRET
COOKIES
❧

Manhattan's king of cookies is clearly **Black Hound** (170 Second Avenue, 979-9505), famous for their teeny-weeny cookies concocted in 20 or so variations: pecan hearts, hazelnut balls, gingerbread people, lemon shortbread, and sandwich hearts — double-decker morsels filled with raspberry or apricot jelly, the perfect gift for a sweetheart. For heartier cookies of the chocolate chip or oatmeal sort, like Mom used to make only much better, get on down to **City Bakery** (22 East 17th Street, 366-1414), which is also famous for its unusual tarts.

SECRET
CREPES
❧

French pancakes rolled around sweet or savory fillings have resurged in popularity lately, with multiple international variations available. My favorite crepes are served at a humble walk-up window in Soho (410 West Broadway, no phone) operated by the excellent **Le Gamin** chain. The number of combinations is blessedly few, and the price is low enough that you can get one for a main course and one for dessert and still spend less than $10. The pancake is made to order on a pair of French appliances inches from your eager nose, and the best is the one filled with chicken breast and Sicilian caponata, a chunky paste of eggplant and tomatoes. A couple of neighboring stores have convenient sills to perch on while you devour.

Also in a Gallic vein is **La Crepe de Bretagne** (46 West 56th Street, 245-4565), although it charges Midtown prices. **Palacinka** (28 Grand Street, 625-0362) appropriates the Czech term for a type of dessert crepe eaten with jelly and applies it to a wide-ranging menu of pancakes filled with mushrooms, ham, eggs, fruits, and cheeses, or, from the sweet side of the fence, Nutella or baked apple with crème fraîche. If you have access to cooking facilities, try the excellent raw blintzes filled with cheese, blueberries, or apples that are sold at the Ukrainian store **Pierogi** at the corner of 7th Street and First Avenue in the East Village.

SECRET
CUBAN SANDWICHES
❧

Thin slices of savory roast pork, ham, and cheese smeared with garlic and oil, spiked with dill-pickle slices, and then annealed in the hot embrace of a two-sided sandwich press to the flatness of a wallet that's been in your back pocket for years: known as the Cuban sandwich, this budget tour de force makes one of the world's greatest quick meals. It was brought to New York by refugees in the early '60s and is available at most of the Cuban lunch counters in the city. The **Havana-Chelsea Luncheonette** (188 Eighth Avenue, 243-9421) offers one of the best, in two sizes: medium ($3) and the belt-busting grande ($4). Also check out their superb octopus salad and "Moors and Christians" — black beans ladled over white rice. Similar Cuban-sandwich excellence is to be found at the **National Café** (210 First Avenue, 473-9354) and **El Mambi** (558 West 181st Street, 568-8321).

SECRET

DANCE LESSONS

Just about anybody can invent free-form dances to rock and roll music, but some of the currently popular exotic and retro styles require instruction and tons of practice. To meet the need a host of institutions have sprung up.

Fueled by the popularity of *River Dance* and *Lord of the Dance*, a pair of shows still traveling throughout the US and Canada, Irish step dancing is now enjoying a vogue that few would have expected. The **Irish Arts Center** (553 West 51st Street, 757-3318) offers eight-session courses geared to beginners that cover your basic reels, jigs, double reels, slip jigs, and so on. To learn swing dances like the Lindy and the Charleston, check out the **New York Swing Society** (598-0154), which presents beginning and advanced classes of varying lengths at 550 Broadway, and sometimes offers single lessons followed by an evening of dancing at various discos around town.

If you just want to learn the fox-trot and other standard ballroom styles, look up **Arthur Murray** in the Yellow Pages — but read on for some more unusual dance lessons. **Broadway Dance** (1733 Broadway, 582-9304) will teach just about any style you might choose, including tap and jazz, while **Anahid Sofian Studio** (29 West 15th Street, 741-2848) specializes in belly dancing. Even more obscure, a Hawaiian-themed store called **Radio Hula** (169 Mercer Street, 226-4467) organizes classes in hula dancing for men and women. **Lezly Skate School** (777-3232) teaches dancing on inline skates, while **Gangani Kathak Dance Company** (586-2684) lists classes in "folk and gypsy dances" as well as kathak, a Northern

Indian dance form. Finally, **Abizaid Arts** (941-8480) features a roster of styles, including jazz, modern, ballet, African, and Brazilian; the school also offers martial-arts instruction.

SECRET

DEATH

✧

New York has nothing like the amazing catacombs of Paris, where the bones of 5,000,000 people are neatly stacked in a former gypsum mine beneath the Fourteenth Arrondissement, and thousands of visitors file through each day, mainly for moral edification. New York, at least, can boast a slew of memento mori, including the **Mother Cabrini Shrine** (701 Fort Washington Avenue, 923-3536), where the bones of the first American saint — with the exception of the skull, which belongs to the Vatican — are enshrined in the altar. Of course, the city's most famous tomb is that of **President Ulysses S. Grant** and his spouse (122nd Street and Riverside Drive), modeled on Napoleon's and outfitted with handsome marble sarcophagi and historically instructive mosaics. It spawned New York's most famous riddle — "Who's buried in Grant's Tomb?" — but the best reason to visit is the panoramic view of the Hudson River afforded by its spectacular location.

The dead had to be dumped somewhere, and many have been consigned to a series of boneyards (see Secret Green Book), of which the largest are in Queens. The drive into Manhattan on the Long Island Expressway passes through **Zion**, **Calvary**, and **New Calvary Cemeteries**, with row upon row of neatly spaced tombstones. From certain angles the graves are juxtaposed against the Manhattan skyline, providing a pithy photo opportunity that's been taken advantage of too many times (for the lazy photographer, also available as a postcard).

Reflecting nineteenth-century German attitudes towards death, there's a restaurant planted improbably in the midst of **Lutheran Cemetery** in the Middle Village section of Queens. Located in a structure that began life in 1854 as a country tavern on the road between the villages of Greenpoint and Jamaica, it was transformed into **Niederstein's** (69–16 Metropolitan Avenue, 718-326-0717) in 1888, and immediately became a hit with mourners from the burgeoning German communities of Sunset Park, Long Island City, and the East Village. On Sunday, the thronged rooms are dotted with black-clad clergy comforting the elderly bereaved in an atmosphere of perpetual hush.

The loveliest of the cemeteries, though, is **Greenwood** (Fifth Avenue and 25th Street, 718-768-7300) in Brooklyn's Sunset Park. Opened in 1840 and comprising 478 acres of rolling hills, it contains Gothic gatehouses, triumphal arches, tombs, cairns, ponds, topiary, and the highest point in Brooklyn, with superb views of New York's upper harbor. It's the final resting place of Currier and Ives, Henry Ward Beecher, Lola Montez, and Samuel F.B. Morse. Guided tours are conducted by **John J. Cashman and Frank Mescall** (718-469-5277); or you can go on your own if you call ahead — walk-ins are not welcome.

If you want to touch and own bones, check out **Evolution** (120 Spring Street, 343-1114) in Soho, which stocks, in addition to butterflies, fossils, and other natural-history artifacts, a fair number of bones, human and animal, faux and true, from entire gorilla skeletons to rattlesnake vertebrae. There are life-size human skeletons (replicas) for $349, and moose horns carved in the shape of, for example, skeletons riding motorcycles for around $1,000. The store used to sell real human bones, but then it got into big trouble. In a similar vein, and much closer to the American Museum of Natural History, is **Maxilla and Mandible** (451 Columbus Avenue, 724-6173).

SECRET
DINERS
※

The diner architecture taken for granted 30 years ago is now an endangered species. The rarest of these — the diner patterned on the old railroad dining car — is the most difficult to locate. Nevertheless, there are still a few left, mainly on the west side of Manhattan in the more hardscrabble commercial zones of Hell's Kitchen and Chelsea. The best of these is **Cheyenne Diner** (411 Ninth Avenue, 465-8750), a streamlined box of undulating aquamarine and chrome offset with pink neon. This diner is only barely self-conscious; its most avid patrons are letter sorters from the nearby postal facility and bikers sporting bandannas on their heads and arm-length tattoos. The elongated dining room makes for plenty of booth seating next to the panoramic windows that offer a view of the city you won't see in the tourist guides. The half-pound burger sided with decent fries and one of those little cups of slaw is a good bet, as are the down-home big feeds like lasagna or meatloaf with mushroom gravy. Striking an oddly modern note are the placards on every table touting buffalo burgers imported from Canada.

More upscale, but still just as attractive, is **Empire Diner** (210 Tenth Avenue, 243-2736), a late-night favorite of drag queens and theater types that dabbles in more ambitious cuisine than the usual diner. There's even a piano in a corner that one of the waiters sometimes plays — mainly show tunes and light classics. It's a fun joint if you sit in the main dining car and not in the next-door annex. Another diner with a hip flair and an ancient facade is **Moondance** (80 Sixth Avenue, 226-1191), so near to Soho that it's hard to believe it still exists.

My favorite diner, though, is Chelsea's **Sam Chinita** (176 Eighth Avenue, 741-0249), an ancient diner that was converted to Cuban-Chinese fare in the distant past. This type of food was brought to New York by immigrants of mixed race who came from Havana in the late '60s. Their ancestors went to Cuba in the '20s from China as indentured servants to cut cane. The diner is a curvy, chromy affair, like an Airstream trailer, and the menu is evenly divided between Cuban and Chinese dishes. The Cuban selections are great; the Chinese awful.

S E C R E T

DOGGIE WORSHIP

❧

Manhattan is an island of dog fanciers who keep the animals for protection as well as companionship. A plethora of dog-oriented institutions has grown up to take advantage of this unique relationship. **The Wagging Tail** (354 Greenwich Street, 285-4900) is one of the newest, offering, in addition to canine grooming, day care, and veterinary services, a rubber-floored doggie party room where you can throw a bash for your pet complete with decorations, piñata, party favors, and a cake shaped like a fire hydrant.

Paws Inn (189 Ninth Avenue, 645-7297) is probably the city's most luxurious pet hotel, sporting a rooftop sundeck and a doggie TV room. **Fetch** (43 Greenwich Avenue, 352-8591) is a new store that specializes in highly designed dog (and cat) accoutrements, including huge plush cushions covered in contrasting leopard-print and carmine fabrics emblazoned with the motto "Good Dog," snack biscuits by Lulu, a first-aid book for hounds, a picture frame with the cut-out word "Woof," and a bowl stenciled "Devil Dog."

Alas, if your pet dies in the New York area, you'll have to consider using the services of **Aldstate** (718-748-8600), a pet crematorium located somewhere in Brooklyn.

SECRET

EGG CREAMS

&

As the Big Apple becomes Disneyfied and McDonaldized, it's harder than ever to find places that serve authentic local specialties. One of the best disappearing treats is the egg cream, a beverage invented by Brooklyn candy merchant Louis Auster in 1890. Containing neither egg nor cream, the beverage is a fizzy version of chocolate milk. The exact proportions of seltzer, chocolate syrup, and milk remain a matter of personal taste and no small controversy. You can still find egg creams at newsstands, soda fountains, and candy shops.

The best in town is at the Ukrainian newsstand between 7th Street and St. Marks on Avenue A, sometimes referred to as **Ray's Candy Shop** even though, in the years I've had egg creams there, I've never encountered anyone named Ray. They squirt the chocolate syrup in first, pour in the milk, and then dribble the soda down a long-handled spoon that twirls in the bottom of the glass. A good white head develops on top of the beverage; the concentration of syrup is greater at the bottom, creating a color gradation from deep brown to white.

The best chocolate syrup to use is Fox's U-Bet, still made in Brooklyn. You can get it in area supermarkets, and it makes a great inexpensive gift for the folks back home. Other places to get exceptionally good egg creams include the East Village's premier newsstand, **Gem Spa** (131 Second Avenue, 529-1146); **Lexington Candy Shop Luncheonette** (1226 Lexington Avenue, 288-0057); **Columbus Circle Pharmacy** (1841 Broadway, 586-8249); **T-Bone Diner** (107–48 Queens Boulevard, Queens, 718-261-7744); and **Junior's** (386 Flatbush Avenue, Brooklyn, 718-852-5257), which also markets an egg-cream kit for $19.95 containing glasses marked to show the amounts of ingredients to use, stirring spoon, and, of course, Fox's U-Bet syrup.

SECRET
ELECTRONICS

❧

My relatives in Texas were surprised to learn that I pay a heck of a lot less for electronic goods than they do, which is odd considering how expensive things are here compared with elsewhere in the US (think groceries, movie tickets, fancy restaurants, housing prices, mixed drinks, taxi rides). The reason for the cheapness of electronics in New York is the huge volume of sales — due partly to visitors and immigrants buying and sending home, and partly to cutthroat competition among retailers.

Avoid like the plague most of the shops selling cameras, boom boxes, computers, stereos, and like merchandise along Fifth Avenue from 28th Street to 59th Street and in the vicinity of Times Square. These stores are the ones tourists are most likely to see, of course. If you must shop at these places, follow these rules: (1) Don't believe the "Going out of Business" signs; (2) Ask to see the warranty before you buy (many of the items sold are "gray goods" — products manufactured for an overseas market and not covered by warranty in the US); (3) Be aware that you may be buying obsolete or discontinued merchandise; (4) Make sure the box is sealed when you buy it, otherwise haggle over the price. One of the good features of these stores is that you can often bargain.

Many of the big chain stores are likewise a pain in the ass, engaging constantly in the "bait and switch" technique, meaning that when you spot a deal in one of its ads, you often find the store is out of that particular item and the sales staff pushes others that they claim are better. Ask a technical question and you'll find the salespeople know nothing. One big electronics discounter that seems to eschew these practices, and has salespeople significantly more knowledgable (example: they look things up on a computer if you ask a question they can't answer), is **J & R Music & Computer World**, located at six addresses across the street from City Hall (15–23 Park Row, 238-9000).

SECRET

EROTIC TOYS

❖

Since the invasion of the bohos, the Lower East Side has never been the same. In the midst of the bodegas, Asian fish markets, and purveyors of Judaica, a number of freakish institutions have sprung up — but this jaded neighborhood has seen it all and takes it in stride. One of the most remarkable new establishments is **Babes in Toyland** (94 Rivington Street, 375-1701), an erotic boutique more comprehensive than any the city has yet seen and devoted to sex-enhancing devices and learning materials with a pleasingly feminist bent, consciously excluding the kind of stupid gag gifts that have heretofore been the stock-in-trade of erotic retailers like Pleasure Chest and Pink Pussycat. The merchandise is roughly divided into categories: vibrators and attachments, dildos, harnesses, butt toys, restraint and sensation toys, cock rings, lubes and safer sex, sexy sundries, videos, books. There are 28 kinds of butt plugs alone, including "lickerish plug" and "voyager 2," most priced in the $10 range. Or go for one of the omnibus collections like the Let's Play Doctor kit ($47). The Web site (www.babeland.com) allows you to preview and order the merchandise, but it's much more fun to visit in person, although I probably wouldn't take someone here on a first date.

SECRET
FARMHOUSES

❖

New York is a city composed entirely of soaring and densely packed skyscrapers, right? It beggars belief, but there are actually farm-houses and cottages remaining in the city, several of them located in Manhattan. You could spend a week touring these structures, many of which are now museums, but why not select a couple and spend a day enjoying the brain-distorting contrast they make with the usual urban architecture? They're also a must for history buffs.

The queen of Manhattan farms is **Dyckman House** (4881 Broadway at 204th Street, 304-9422), located in the uppermost Inwood section of Manhattan and easily accessible by subway. This lovely porched and gambrel-roofed structure was built by William Dyckman in 1748 on lands owned by his grandfather. It was burned by the British during the Revolutionary War and rebuilt in 1783. Fully restored in 1915, it contains Dutch and English period furnishings that reflect the spartan quality of life in the eighteenth century.

Also originally built in 1748, the mansion of a country squire rather than a simple farmhouse, is **Van Cortlandt Manor** (Broadway near 242nd Street, Bronx, 718-543-3344). This handsome fieldstone structure contains fancy furnishings by Chippendale, Delft, and Whieldon, and stands in the midst of Revolutionary battlefields — in fact, George Washington conducted a campaign from the premises. In spite of the undeniable appeal of its wealth and history, Van Cortlandt Manor was also a working farm where cattle were raised, and flax and other crops were sown for at least a century. The adjacent park, formed from the farmstead, has a bird sanctuary, nature walks, a swimming pool, and one of the city's few cricket pitches, favored by West Indian sportspeople. The site is easily accessible by subway.

Built as a carriage house in 1799 (though converted to residential use in 1826), the **Abigail Adams Smith Museum** (421 East 61st Street, 980-9352) is incongruously located next to the approach to the Queensboro Bridge on Manhattan's East Side. The structure was associated with a much larger estate house that was demolished. Nevertheless, it makes a startling contrast with the surrounding buildings. Run as a museum of colonial-era furnishings, the house is maintained by the Colonial Dames of America. Don't miss the eighteenth-century garden.

To see how the other half lived, seek out the **Sven Bernard House** at the corner of Charles and Greenwich Streets in the West Village. This minuscule, white-frame structure was built sometime in the nineteenth century on the Upper East Side of Manhattan as a backhouse — a small cottage occupying the strip of land that remained after a larger structure was built on the street. The house was moved at least twice before it arrived at its current location, and it is one of the few remaining examples of a slapdash style of vernacular domestic architecture.

Other notable rural estates still standing include the **Bartow-Pell Mansion** (Shore Road, Pelham Bay Park, Bronx, 718-885-1461), built sometime around 1840 in the European château style and remarkable for its elaborately landscaped grounds; and the **Kingsland House** (143–35 37th Avenue, Flushing, Queens, 718-939-0647), a gigantic farmhouse in the Dutch style dating from 1774, also notable for the beautiful weeping beech tree on its grounds.

Straining credibility, there is still one semiworking farm within the city limits of New York, and, as you might expect, the **Queens County Farm Museum** (73–50 Little Neck Parkway, Floral Park, Queens, 718-347-FARM) has been turned into something of a tourist trap. It bills itself as the oldest continually cultivated site in the state, and even though its puny 47 acres can't match some of the 500-acre behemoths upstate there still seems to be a lot of growin' goin' on. The 1771 Flemish-style farmhouse is in a good state of preservation, but most of the outbuildings date from the 1920s, when the grounds were used as an activity area for psychiatric patients. Hayrides are available on weekends, and the farm operates a produce stand during summer and fall. The museum is open year-round.

SECRET
FERRIES

Beginning in the early nineteenth century and continuing until the late 1950s, numerous ferries crisscrossed the rivers from Brooklyn, Queens, and New Jersey to Manhattan. Supplanted by tunnels and bridges, these routes fell into disuse. Now the ferries are returning as crossing by tunnels and bridges has become increasingly difficult due to extreme overcrowding.

Departing from Battery Park City in Lower Manhattan, **NY Waterway** (1-800-53-FERRY, Web site: www.nywaterway.com) passenger ferries cross the Hudson to Hoboken and two locations in Jersey City on a schedule of frequent departures beginning around 6:30 A.M. and running until almost 10 P.M. Priced at $2 each way, a ferry ride is an excellent way to enjoy the river, visit some interesting Jersey neighborhoods, and ogle some commuting Wall Streeters (if you're so inclined). New service has recently been added between Pier 78 (38th Street) in Manhattan and Port Royal in New Jersey. On the Queens side, there's a ferry from Hunter's Point to East 34th Street. Free shuttle buses operate in Manhattan to and from the departure points — call the information number listed above for schedules.

The **Staten Island Ferry** (225-5368), a line operating continuously since 1884 with several magnificent boats, each carrying as many as 6,000 passengers, is the best travel bargain in the city — it's free in both directions. Traversing the 6.2 miles of the Upper Bay in this manner is the best way to view the Statue of Liberty and Ellis Island in context. The ferry operates 24 hours per day (although in the wee hours departures occur only once hourly) and departs from Battery Park in Manhattan and St. George in Staten Island.

S E C R E T
FIREFIGHTING
✤

Known as "New York's Bravest," the city's firefighters have had an illustrious history beginning with the first volunteer brigade, organized by the General Assembly in 1737 in response to a spate of fires caused by faulty chimneys and accelerated by construction of new dwellings with wood instead of the traditional stone and brick. The brigade's equipment consisted of a pair of Newsham hand pumpers imported from London.

But the history has also been a chaotic one. During the eighteenth century and much of the nineteenth, fire brigades remained volunteer, headquartered in bars and closely aligned with political factions like Tammany Hall. Brawls broke out when competing brigades arrived at a fire, and the city suffered a series of calamitous blazes. A 1776 conflagration obliterated nearly 500 homes, one third of the city. The Great Fire of 1835 wiped out 674 buildings on Wall, Broad, and South Streets, while the Great Fire of 1845 razed 300 structures in the same vicinity. Accusations that firefighters were setting fires as well as putting them out led to the appointment of the first professional firefighting force in 1865. Concurrently, a system of bell towers was erected all over town to facilitate rapid response.

The **New York City Fire Museum** (278 Spring Street, 691-1303, adults $4, children $2) recounts the history of New York firefighters. Situated in a three-story former firehouse — Engine Company #30 — the collection includes both horse-drawn and engine-powered vehicles, paintings, toys, uniforms, commemorative plaques, and other diverting artifacts. All around town, working firehouses provide informal tours if their employees are not too busy and you ask nicely. **Engine Company #18** (132 West 10th Street, 570-4218), constructed in 1891, is a particular favorite, featuring a single fire engine and four brass poles that the firefighters slide down. The last remaining **fire tower** in the city stands in Harlem's Mount Morris Park. Dating from 1856, it's an open-sided octagonal structure of cast iron with a curving, vertigo-inducing stairway; the huge bell is still attached halfway up. The park is ringed with Victorian-era houses that are worth a look on their own.

New York Firefighter's Friend (263 Lafayette Street, 226-3142) peddles a broad range of firefighting paraphernalia, some of it genuine — including used black slickers, boots, and helmets. They also sell sloganed T-shirts and a selection of toys, like stuffed animals and fire trucks. You can order via their Web site (www.nyfirestore. com), as well.

S E C R E T

FISHING

❧

Not a day goes by that I don't see a fisherman — pole under arm and tackle box in hand — trudging down 23rd Street towards the East River or riding the N train to Coney Island. New York is a city of fishermen, and the fact that most of them are fishing to feed their families rather than for sport or relaxation should only enhance your interest in watching them, or in picking up a pole and joining in. Of course there are periodic warnings about chemicals in the fish, but those warnings usually take the form of, "Don't eat fish you've caught around New York more than once a week."

For duffers and children, there's Central Park's **Harlem Meer**, up in the northeast corner near 110th Street. It, like all the lakes in Central

Park, is stocked with fish on a regular basis, but here they lend you fishing equipment for free. The catch is that once you catch a fish you have to throw it back in. **Prospect Park Lake** in Brooklyn and **Meadow Lake** in the Flushing Meadows-Corona Park section of Queens are other popular stocked fishing holes in city parks. Your most likely catch is small sunfish, carp, or catfish.

The **Hudson River Conservancy** (353-0366) conducts a fishing program every Saturday and Sunday from noon until 5:30 PM, providing fishing lessons and free equipment in addition to instruction in the kinds of fish and other fauna and flora that are native to the Hudson. The program is conducted at Pier 25, a couple blocks north of Chambers Street.

But if you're an angler out for more substantial fish, go to the **East River**. There you'll see people fishing from the 90s in Carl Shurz Park down to East River Park, where substantial bluefish, blackfish, fluke, and striped bass are often caught. The **Steeplechase Pier** (that's the big one sticking way out into the water) at Coney Island is another fishing hot spot, especially for fluke and porgy. In summer and fall, fluke is a popular catch among passengers aboard the 16 party-fishing boats that set out from Brooklyn's **Sheepshead Bay** from the quay along Emmons Avenue. They set sail, figuratively speaking, at anywhere from 7:30 to 9:30 in the morning, although afternoon and evening expeditions are sometimes offered. The boats typically hold 25 to 50 anglers and drop anchor in the ocean right off of Staten Island. Excursions average $32 for a full day or $16 for a half, and bait, rods, and tackle are provided. Boats that accept telephone reservations include **Sea Queen II** (718-646-6224), **Pastime Princess** (718-252-4398), **Miss Nel** (718-891-0337), and **Explorer** (718-680-2207), which also books 24-hour tuna-fishing marathons. Most boats have a snack bar, TV lounge, and other luxuries.

The Sheepshead Bay fleet, believe it or not, is popular with sashimi fanatics, who go especially for the fluke. They dress the fish the minute it's caught and tuck right into the shimmering white flesh. A very kinky food scene. Bluefish are also snagged during this season, but they don't make very good sashimi. Winter catches include cod and other fish in the same family. By the way, if you luck out and catch some fish, almost any of the restaurants along Emmons Avenue will cook them for you for a reasonable fee of $5 or $10.

Fishermen agree that **Capitol Bait and Tackle** (218 West 23rd Street, 929-6132) is one of the city's best sources for fishing equipment, be it for freshwater, saltwater, or fly fishing. **Manhattan Custom Tackle** (913 Broadway, 505-6690) is more upscale, custom building rods that are more substantial than off-the-rack varieties. For a quick and cheap fix of fishing equipment, try either of the Manhattan **K-Marts** (1 Pennsylvania Plaza — just north of Penn Station — 760-1188; 770 Broadway — facing Astor Place — 673-1540), which have fishing displays far more extensive than you'd ever expect to see in New York — probably because so many New Yorkers look to angling to reduce their food bills.

S E C R E T
FLATBUSH
❖

Though Brooklyn's Flatbush (meaning "level forest" in Dutch) was established in 1652, it remained a rural settlement until the 1880s, when the Brooklyn, Flatbush and Coney Island Railroad (nowadays the D train) made it easily accessible from Manhattan. By the time it was annexed by the City of Brooklyn in 1894, it was well on the way to becoming a suburb. In the 1920s, Jews escaping the urban squalor of Manhattan's Lower East Side settled there and created a great tradition, including the dialect of English that came to be known as Brooklynese.

Since the 1960s, Flatbush has been a haven for English- and French-speaking Caribbean immigrants, mainly from Jamaica, Trinidad, Guyana, and Haiti. They've brought to this neighborhood of single-family homes and modest apartment houses a vibrant and colorful street culture, including Caribbean-style open-air markets, excellent cheap restaurants, and shops that sell a range of exotic items. A visit to Flatbush is like a cheap vacation to Kingston or Port of Spain.

The main axis for English-speaking islanders is Flatbush Avenue, which also boasts many of the area's architectural landmarks. Just south of Church Avenue is the neo-Gothic **Erasmus Hall High School** (1903), whose alumni include Barbara Streisand and chess master Bobby Fischer. The central courtyard wraps around the 1786 clapboard **Erasmus Hall Academy**, one of the oldest schools in the United States, now a museum (718-282-7804). Other landmarks include the 1876 **Flatbush Town Hall** (35 Snyder Avenue between Flatbush and Bedford) and, across the street from Erasmus High, the 1853 **Flatbush Dutch Reformed Church**, notable for its Georgian-Federal-Tuscan mixture of architectural styles.

But the Caribbean institutions are what make this neighborhood a must visit. Begin at **Danny and Pepper** (771 Flatbush Avenue, 718-284-9187) for some of the best jerk chicken in town, a recipe the Jamaicans inherited from the Arawak Indians, which involves rubbing the bird with a piquant mixture of herbs and spices and grilling it over charcoal. Also don't miss the fried dough called festival. Danny and Pepper is strictly carryout, so eat as you walk or picnic in nearby **Prospect Park** (one block north and one block west).

Just down the street is **Miracle Warehouse** (841 Flatbush Avenue, 718-941-2100), the city's largest botanica — an establishment that sells the articles required for practicing the religion variously known as santeria, vodun, or voodoo. Within this religion, aspects of Catholicism, including the use of saint figures and candles, have been merged with African forms of natural religion or animism. Miracle Warehouse is liberally stocked with every kind of candle, incense, herb, devotional oil, and magical paraphernalia imaginable. In addition, three advisers in full santeria regalia are available at all times, and don't be discouraged by the disclaimer posted at the register: "For entertainment purposes only."

Hungryman's (829 Flatbush Avenue, 718-940-8801) specializes in rotis, the burrito-style wrap made with a flatbread called dahl poorie brought to the Caribbean by East Indian immigrants and popular on all the English-speaking islands. Fillings include chicken curry, conch, goat, and potato, or just vegetables. Nearby **Guyana Roti House** (3021 Church Avenue, 718-940-9413) specializes in the same quick meal, with the addition of a range of tasty Guyanese snacks including codfish cakes, tamarind balls, and mittai — little fingers of fried dough coated with sugar and cinnamon. Directly across the street from Hungryman's is one of the larger **open-air markets**, with stalls selling frilly pastel dresses for girls, batik fabrics, cosmetics, cassette tapes, Indian-style multilevel lunch pails, and Trinidadian snacks like chana (roasted chickpeas) and preserved mango colored an unearthly shade of red.

Nostrand Avenue, parallel to Flatbush and a few blocks east, is the main axis for the Haitian community. The best place to sample Franco-Caribbean food is **YoYo Fritaille** (1758 Nostrand Avenue,

718-469-7460), where red neon signs sputter "YOYO," and a yellow overhang offers "Bega, Acra, Marinade, Lambi, Tassot, Banane, Patate." Most of the offerings at this lunch counter fall into the category of "fritaille," or fried things. One specialty is griot (pronounced "gree-oh"), made from chunks of pork first marinated in garlic, shallots, spices, and bitter orange; then boiled until the liquid evaporates; and finally fried, which further anneals the ingredients to the surface. The result is a chewy exterior, a moist interior, and intensely concentrated flavors. Just down the street at Nostrand and Newkirk, right across the street from the griffined and crenellated **St. Jerome Church**, a line of open-air vendors hawks fresh herbs, sea moss, frankincense, and hairbrushes. Finish your tour of Flatbush with a visit to **Taste of the Tropics** (see Secret Ice Cream).

SECRET

FLEA MARKETS

❧

What's the appeal of a flea market? Surely not the selection, which could be bettered by any specialty mart, or the prices, which can seem hilariously high, especially if you don't have the slightest interest in the object in question. Maybe it's because flea markets confirm our assumptions about the unpredictable nature of the universe — they juxtapose cast-off merchandise in illogical ways with inadvertent artistry.

Sooner or later, every square inch of the city finds its best use, and the parking lots along **Sixth Avenue in the Flower District** are no exception. This ancient zone, where wholesale flowers from around the world are peddled on weekdays (see Secret Flower

District), used to empty out on weekends and become a ghost town. The first flea market started modestly at the corner of 25th Street a decade ago, operating on Saturdays and Sundays. The original market is still there, but now it's two blocks long and includes hundreds of vendors. The first market was wildly popular; others soon sprang up in the area and in a couple of other parts of town. It has become a favorite weekend occupation of New Yorkers to visit these open-air markets, often with no intention of buying anything, just to admire the array of nostalgic items and enjoy the fine weather.

I spent a recent afternoon strolling the flea markets, and here are my notes. The market from **24th to 26th Streets** is now two separate establishments. Admission to the south one is free, and typical of its merchandise are used watchbands, costume jewelry, Santa Claus mugs, 45 r.p.m. records, used bikes in the $50-to-$150 range, black-and-white snapshots from the '40s, metal molds used to make doll heads, and pseudoantique brass signs with inscriptions like "No Cocaine Peddling," perfect for home or office.

The block to the north charges a $1 admission fee. Though I generally wouldn't pay the dollar on principle, this time I did, and this is what I saw: old-looking rings in glass cases, some particularly ugly vases, toys from the '30s, quasi-pornographic matchbook covers, straight razors, blue glass, Middle Eastern rugs, and cigar-label printing plates.

Across the street and up one block (**27th Street and Sixth Avenue**) is another flea market on an L-shaped lot selling used aquariums, a child's John Deere riding tractor, eight '50s dinette chairs in perfect condition that seemed like a bargain at $200 for the lot, glassware, children's clothes, and medical illustrations suitable for framing — including a tapeworm and a sideways view of the female endocrine system.

Along **25th Street to the west of Sixth Avenue**, a couple of indoor markets have been spawned by the outdoor market. These feature more expensive collectibles and actual antiques (defined by the federal government as being at least 100 years old), which are more carefully presented and organized. At **Chelsea Antiques Building** (110 West 25th Street, 929-0909), for example, one shop is devoted exclusively to Pez dispensers, old and new, from England, Israel, Russia, and several other countries. You can pay as much as $100 for one of these cute trinkets.

At **Seventh Avenue and 25th Street** is another free open-air market that seems to have escaped from the cluster on Sixth Avenue. Here the merchandise is a little less expensive and the vendors more ragtag; they specialize in books, scruffy furniture, and bad framed art. Soho boasts its own major parking-lot market at **Broadway and Grand**, where the selection of items for sale seems influenced by nearby Canal Street; used calculators and electronic equipment are among the offerings. There are also several African vendors selling beads and handwoven fabrics, and a stall hawking old children's games like Bruce Jenner's Decathalon Game and Dizzy Dinosaur. The browsers at this market are younger, more artistic types, and it's hard to tell if the stall that sells huge crescent wrenches and other outsized steamfitter's apparatus is offering them as tools or as objets d'art.

S E C R E T
FLOWER DISTRICT
✤

In nineteenth-century New York, merchants pursuing the same trade would congregate in specialized commercial zones, like guilds in medieval cities. Many of these districts have been obliterated by urban renewal, but — thankfully — others persist despite the passage of time. Rug merchants — many of them Persian Jews and Shiite Muslims who emigrated to New York in the 1920s — inhabit the blocks north of Madison Square in the high 20s and low 30s. Furriers can still be found on 29th and 30th Streets in Chelsea, while the Garment District, extending from 34th to 40th Street, between Sixth and Ninth Avenues, is the largest and most successful of these remaining special zones. (Dig especially the shops that specialize in buttons and trimmings on the east side of Sixth Avenue starting at 34th Street and moving northward.)

The most pleasant of these commercial neighborhoods is the **Flower District**, comprised of Sixth Avenue between 27th and 29th Streets and the block of 28th Street to the west. Flowers, corn plants, potted palms, and rococo planters are trundled out into the common thoroughfare, and if the weather is warm, you'll feel like you're hiking through the jungle. Most of the shops have the words "Wholesale Only" or "To the Trade" emblazoned on their windows, but this is partly a sales-tax dodge. Represent yourself as a designer, photographer, or photo stylist, and chances are they'll sell you an armload of calla lilies, azaleas, or even fragrant honeysuckle, depending on the season, for a price ranging from $6 to $15 — about one quarter of what you'd expect to pay at the florist. Even more important, the flowers are bizarrely fresh.

To the east in the blocks surrounding Broadway is a wholesale district crammed with outlets selling made-in-Asia trinkets by the dozen. Nevertheless, you — a retail customer — are welcome in any of these joints, as long as you buy in multiples of twelve. When it comes to key chains and hair clips, a dozen won't cost you much more than you'd expect to pay for just one in a retail store. The merchants are mainly Indian and Korean, and there are plenty of cheap Indian chop houses in the vicinity, such as **Kashmiri Kebab** (11 West 29th Street, 684-4444), and even a Senegalese cafe, **N'Gone** (215 West 28th Street, 244-0390), so located because African street vendors are important customers in this wholesale district.

SECRET
FRENCH FRIES
❧

Golden-brown fingers of fried potato — commonly known as french fries — were really invented in Belgium, although short-story writer O. Henry, himself a longtime New York resident, apparently invented the term. Anyway, french fries are always popular here, and recently there's been a fad for Belgian-style fries, twice fried in oil and served with a variety of sauces in a paper cone. First was **Pommes Frites Authentic Belgian Fries** (123 Second Avenue, 674-1234) in the East Village, where upwards of 30 crazy sauces are routinely available from an ever-changing roster that always includes Dutch fritesauce, a kind of wet mayonnaise favored in the Low Countries, and, of course, ketchup. Opened more recently, and offering fewer sauces, **Le Frite Kot** (148 West 4th Street, 979-2616) actually has slightly better fries; not quite so brown as the Pommes Frites product and a little more potatoey. You can also get good Belgian fries, though not in a paper cone, at the three locations of **Petit Abeille** (107 West 18th Street, 604-9350; 400 West 14th Street, 727-1505; and 466 Hudson Street, 741-6479), tiny Belgian bistros.

S E C R E T
GARDENS
✤

New York isn't exactly a garden paradise, but there are a lot more public gardens than you'd imagine, perhaps more concentrated with flowers than equivalent gardens elsewhere due to the limited square footage available. Some are designated **"viewing gardens,"** meaning that you can only peer in through the fence. The best of these is behind the spired courthouse, now a public library, at **Sixth Avenue and 10th Street**. The garden itself occupies a plot of land that was once a women's prison; a friend remembers when inmates used to lower little baskets on strings, hoping to cadge cigarettes from passersby. The garden has been recently refitted with a grand wrought-iron fence, and the flower beds can be viewed from three adjacent streets. There's another good viewing garden at **West 4th Street and LaGuardia Place** right in front of a supermarket. Just south of that, at **LaGuardia and Houston Street**, is a fenced plot of land that claims to present the flora of Manhattan before the Europeans arrived. Judge for yourself.

The decimation of the Lower East Side and parts of the East Village by fire and building condemnation in the mid-1970s (this part of town was gradually becoming a South-Bronx-style slum), before it became high-priced real estate, triggered the emergence of a gardening movement. It all began with the **Liz Christy Garden** at the corner of Houston Street and the Bowery in 1974. A series of community gardens are now mainly overseen by an organization called **Green Guerrillas** (625 Broadway, 674-814) and are typically rented from the city for a fee of $1 per year. The gardens are divided into small plots (four-by-eight feet), which are worked by individuals

who pay about $12 or so each year for the privilege. Some grow vegetables, some grow flowers, and some build magnificent earthworks covered with exotic vegetation. Strolling through one of these gardens is an exhilarating experience — many put as much effort into their small plots as suburban gardeners put into areas 20 times larger. One of the oldest and most developed of these is the **6th and B Garden**, located at 6th Street and Avenue B in the Alphabetland section of the East Village. An ancient willow presides over the huge spread, which contains an herb garden, a gigantic sculpture covered with stuffed animals and other found objects, an amphitheater, mature fruit trees (the fruit's free for the taking), and over 100 individual plots. There are free music and poetry performances and free film screenings in the evenings from about the first of April to the middle of October, but you must visit the garden to examine the current monthly calendar.

Central Park is loaded with beautiful outdoor minienvironments, but none is more stunning than the rarely visited **Conservatory Garden** (Fifth Avenue and 103rd Street), approached from the avenue via a wrought-iron gate that used to grace one of Andrew Carnegie's mansions farther downtown. A promenade leads to a pair of sweeping stairways that ascend to a trellised overlook; here cotillions for the rich were held in the long-ago. Down below are two symmetrical gardens dotted with shaded benches under overhanging trees. This hideaway is Central Park's best-kept secret, and the spacious, well-maintained rest rooms are a bonus.

The **New York Horticultural Society** (128 West 58th Street, 757-0915) has a well-stocked library for the use of members ($15 per year) and offers classes in city gardening, flower arranging, and other gardenological topics.

SECRET

GAY

✣

New York and San Francisco are the gay capitals of the world, and it would take a whole book to detail the richness of New York's queer empire. It began in Greenwich Village a century ago when the docks were a cruising ground for same-sex encounters, but has extended northward during the last decade into Chelsea and Hell's Kitchen as a result of the real-estate pressures that have turned the Village into a sanctuary for the wealthy. A gay walking tour will include an amble down Christopher Street from Sixth Avenue to Hudson, and thence northward along Hudson till it turns into Eighth Avenue, and finally up Eighth to 23rd Street.

Sights on Christopher include the **Oscar Wilde Memorial Bookstore** (15 Christopher Street, 255-8097), which stocks plenty of souvenirs of the neighborhood, and **Stonewall** (53 Christopher Street, 463-0950), the bar where, 30 years ago, a police raid targeting homosexuals spawned the modern gay-rights movement. At adjacent **Sheraton Square** is the world's first gay outdoor sculpture. For those inclined to S & M, a number of leather shops dot the blocks of Christopher to the west, and there's also the **Original Espresso Bar** (82 Christopher Street, 627-3870), a predominantly gay and lesbian coffee shop known for its excellent brews and sandwiches.

Hudson Street and Eighth Avenue, too, have more than their share of gay-affiliated businesses, as do many of the side streets. Popular restaurants in this corridor include **Candy Bar** (131 Eighth Avenue, 229-9702), serving surprisingly good food, and **Manatus** (340 Bleecker Street, 989-7042) and **Hudson Corner** (570 Hudson Street, 229-2727) — both of which are far better for boy-watching than for their diner-style food. Lesbians chow down at **Rubyfruit Bar & Grill** (see Secret Lesbians).

Over the frontier of 14th Street in Chelsea, **Big Cup** (228 Eighth Avenue, 206-0059) is the fave coffee bar, while **Different Light** (151 West 19th Street, 989-4850) is the center of the gay literary universe; here readings and other events are frequently held. **Splash** (50 West 17th Street, 691-0073) is a favorite area bar.

Detailing all the gay nightclubs is beyond the scope of this book, and, anyway, most of the action takes the form of gay-themed nights at clubs that often shift from month to month. The meat-packing district — along the westernmost stretch of 14th Street — is a particular hot spot, with clubs like **Hell** (59 Gansevoort Street, 727-1666) and **Mother** (432 West 14th Street, 366-5680), but the best way to find out about current nightlife is to scan the free gay and lesbian publications available in boxes throughout the Village and Chelsea: *lgny (Lesbian & Gay New York)* and *New York Blade*, both tabloids, and miniature magazines *HX*, *HX for Her*, *Twist*, and *Next*. Michael Musto's weekly column in the *Village Voice* is also a must-read, and *Time Out New York* has a special section for gay events.

SECRET

GOLF

❖

No, you can't play in Manhattan. There aren't any golf courses. But you can get pretty damn close. There's no driving range in the world more spectacular than the **Golf Club at Chelsea Piers** (Pier 59, 336-6400), where you can hit balls from four ascending levels that furnish marvelous views of the Hudson River and the bucolic Jersey Shore. I always pick the uppermost level because then I can hit the balls farther onto the Astroturf pier while experiencing a mild feeling of vertigo. And I double my pleasure by going right at sunset. If I'm in a vindictive mood, I aim at the little car that drives up and down the pier gathering balls, one hundred of which will set you back $15. This seems expensive until you consider that the million-dollar view is included (so is the golf-club rental, if you didn't bring your own). There's no time limit, so you can hit the balls very slowly. Another enjoyable aspect is the Japanese-made delivery system that pulls the rubber tee into the mat between strokes and automatically tees up the ball — you never have to touch it at all! There's also a pro shop on the premises if you want to buy a snazzy golf outfit before starting in on your bucket.

There are plenty of places in Manhattan that offer golf equipment. Real golfers swear by **Richard Metz Golf Studio** (425 Madison Avenue, 759-6940). Here — in addition to bags, shoes, apparel, balls, and clubs — there are driving cages and putting greens where lessons are conducted: $350 for a series of 10. **World of Golf** (147 East 47th Street, 755-9398) discounts the usual golf equipment and accessories.

There are golf courses in the other boroughs, several open to the public and surprisingly affordable. Staten Island's **La Tourette Golf Course** (1001 Richmond Hill Road, 718-351-1889) is municipally owned and takes advantage of the island's rolling terrain; a round costs $18.50, slightly more than a dollar per hole. Unfortunately, it's virtually inaccessible without a car. Pelham Bay Park in the Bronx boasts two publicly owned courses, **Split Rock** and **Pelham**, both sharing the same information hotline (718-885-1258). And if your golf bag has wheels, you can walk the half mile from the R subway to Brooklyn's **Dyker Beach Golf Course** (Seventh Avenue and 86th Street, 718-836-9722), which enjoys a breezy maritime location. Fore!

SECRET
GONDOLA
✤

The city's oddest form of transportation is not the tram (see Secret Tramway), or Central Park's horse-drawn carriages, but the gondola. The pricey **Park View Restaurant**, next to the Loeb Boathouse on Central Park's "the Lake," offers half-hour gondola rides from 5 till 10 each evening. A half-hour jaunt on the tree-shaded, wooden-bridged, and many-branched lake runs $30, but the boat will hold as many as six. As an added bonus, the boatman — in Venetian costume — sings opera arias as he poles along. Weather permitting, rides begin in April and are still offered as late as November. Call 517-2233 for reservations.

Cheaper are the rowboat rentals at the **Loeb Boathouse**, which cost $10 an hour (with a $20 deposit); the boats hold five people. They are available from 10 A.M. until only 5 P.M., probably so you won't harass the gondolier by following him all over the lake. While we're on the subject of boating, Hudson River kayaking is available at the **Sports Center at Chelsea Piers** (West 23rd Street and West Side Highway, 336-6068). There is a prerequisite, however: you have to take a pair of two-hour kayaking lessons — the first in a pool, the second between the piers — to qualify for supervised excursions. The most ambitious of these is a circumnavigation of Manhattan, a 25-mile row that takes as long as nine hours. Kayak info is also available at the Chelsea Piers Web site (www.chelseapiers.com).

Free kayaking clinics are offered by the **Hudson River Conservancy** on weekends from May to October at the **Downtown Boathouse** (Pier 26, 966-1852 or 254-1338), and they provide the kayaks.

S E C R E T

GOTHIC

The city's most impressive Gothic revival structure is **Grace Church** at 10th Street and Broadway, its elaborate, soaring tower visible from many points downtown. The church was designed by James Renwick Jr. (who had studied the notebooks of English Gothic architects) and was completed in 1845; the attached rectory was finished a year later. Viewing the church is an overwhelming experience, heightened by contrast — the structure is surrounded by blah commercial buildings. It's as if a little bit of heaven had fallen from the sky. Also, don't miss the three church house buildings around the corner on Fourth Avenue, now used as a private school, mainly for wealthy children.

Other buildings by Renwick include the bi-towered **St. Patrick's Cathedral** at Fifth Avenue and 50th Street (completed in 1879), also in the Gothic style. Catholic or not, you are welcome to enter and wander the sanctuary almost anytime during the day. Brooklyn's **Greenwood Cemetery** is also rich in Gothic structures (see Secret Death), and don't forget the towers of the city's most famous bridge (see Secret Brooklyn Bridge).

SECRET
GREEN BOOK
❧

Every couple of years, New York City publishes the *Green Book*, a comprehensive phone and address book for every branch of city government. Despite its compact size, it's a dangerous tome, not only furnishing access to city offices and functionaries nobody knew existed but also providing a bird's-eye view of the most complex urban bureaucracy in the country. Furthermore, it provides perfect browsing material for the amateur sociologist. The section entitled "Correction Department" contains the following Dickensian paragraph:

> Potter's Field
> Hart Island, Bronx 10464

> The Administrative Code (Sec 21–110) provides that the Potter's Field on Hart Island shall be under the control of the Dept. of Correction, and the burial of deceased paupers therein shall continue under rules and regulations established by joint action of the Departments of Social Services and Correction, or in the case of disagreement between such departments, under such regulations as may be established by the Mayor.

The book is, of course, tremendously practical as well. In it find the hotline for special events in the parks (360-3456), the Commission on Human Rights' discrimination complaint number (NO-2 BIAS), as well as the phone number for emergency poisoning treatment (POISONS); and get instructions on how to file a health complaint about a restaurant (442-9666).

Naturally, the city doesn't make it easy to acquire this volume. Get the 605-page book for $15 at **City Books** (2223 Municipal Building, 669-8245), where they sell a number of other city-related titles that you can't get elsewhere, including *Big Apple Street Smarts*, edited by Robert Persky, and *Country Days in New York City*, by Divya Symmers.

S E C R E T

GUITARS

❖

Between Sixth and Seventh Avenues, 48th Street is a mecca for guitar enthusiasts. The stretch houses several music stores that sell the latest guitars, basses, keyboards, amps, PA systems, and studio equipment. **Manny's** (156 West 48th Street, 819-0578) is the most upscale, and consequently the most likely place to spot rock stars, while **Sam Ash** (155 West 48th Street, 719-2625) has bloated into several storefronts by giving off-price deals on musical equipment.

Much more charming is the downtown institution **Matt Umanov** (273 Bleecker Street, 675-2157), where, in addition to the latest Gibson Les Paul variations, you can check out 70-year-old Dobros and Gretsches on one hand and cheap Strat copies on the other. For just the right Dan Electro, go straight to **Mojo Guitars** (102 St. Marks Place, 260-7751), where incredible bargains can often be had and the stars of East Village rock periodically drop in. A few years back, I bought a blond Music Man bass for a mere $290, only to find a few years later that its value had escalated to more than

$2,000. Forget stocks and bonds — investing in vintage musical instruments is the way to really make a pile!

An even more out-of-the-way place to buy a vintage ax is **30th Street Guitars** (236 West 30th Street, 868-2660). Pawnshops also carry them, but at drastically inflated prices. Who'd have figured?

SECRET
GUJARATI VILLAGE

❖

Many recent immigrants from India come from the western state of Gujarat, where the surname Patel abounds and vegetarians vastly outnumber meat eaters. **Vatan** (409 Third Avenue, 689-5666) is a Gujarati restaurant made to look like a turn-of-the-century Indian village with thatched huts, a spreading banyan tree, and a white-washed colonial building; inside are a pair of rooms that look out onto the "village," and a rooftop seating area with Indian-style tables, recommended only for the limber. But my favorite table is under the tree.

You don't need a menu because on offer is a single, strictly vegetarian meal ($19.95) of several courses, including miniature poori with chick peas and yogurt, several dry-cooked vegetable stews, a fritter or two, and a rib-sticking casserole of rice and chickpeas with a savory gravy. At any stage of the meal you may ask for more of anything. A glass of scented tea rounds out the repast, and you'll never notice you weren't eating meat.

SECRET
HEALTH CLUBS

✤

One of the first questions my buff out-of-town friends ask me when they hit the city is, "Where can I work out?" I first tell them about the **New York Health and Racquet Club** chain, with multiple locations (39 Whitehall Street, 269-9800; 24 East 13th Street, 924-4600; 20 East 50th Street, 593-1500; 110 West 56th Street, 541-1700), where you can use the facilities — including microscopic swimming pools — for $50 a day. If this seems steep, and the friend is staying awhile, I reveal that the **Executive Fitness Center** at the Vista Hotel (3 World Trade Center, 466-9266), will sell you a one-month membership for $135. If this provokes further consternation, I let the cat out of the bag.

New York City maintains a vast network of public gyms, including **Carmine Street** (Clarkson Street and 7th Avenue South, 242-5228), which boasts basketball courts, ping-pong tables, circular jogging track, progressive resistance machines, stationary bicycles, and a weight room. The cost? Just $25 *per year*, and no proof of residence is required, although you must pay by check or money order (the latter of which may be purchased from any bank, post office, or check-cashing business — there's one in nearly every neighborhood). Sure, these facilities were built in the '30s and they're a little funky, but I consider the mix of users (gay and straight, young and old, male and female, well-off and financially disadvantaged) to be one of the best reasons to go. Plus, I like the architecture at every one of these facilities. The pool at **Asser Levy** (23rd Street and Asser Levy Place, 447-2020), for example, is a masterpiece based on the German natatorium model, with high ceilings and a lion head spouting water. Another favorite is the unimaginatively named **East 54th Street Recreation Center** (348 East 54th Street, 397-3154). Check the blue (government) pages of the phone book for a complete list. One membership entitles you to use any recreation center in the city.

S E C R E T
HEMP
❧

You thought I was going to tell you where to buy pot? Not likely. Instead, I'll direct you to its lesser-known use — as a hip material to make just about anything you can imagine. This contemporary fad, seemingly eco-conscious, has spawned a store called — you guessed it — **Hemp** (423 Broome Street, 965-0500, Web site: www.planethemp.com). There you can find blue jeans, stationery, mouse pads, wallets, suitcases, and candles (wick only) — all made of hemp. The baseball caps ($19.95), with such logos as an upside-down cow, a lotus flower, or "Farmy," carry the imprecation, "Caution: Do Not Try to Smoke This Cap." Agrarian hippie chic.

S E C R E T
HIDDEN RESTAURANTS
❧

The common wisdom is that restaurants need a great location and appealing signage to succeed. Even then, they're lucky if they last five years. Taking the opposite tack, some restaurants hide from public view down narrow alleys or in obscure corners, forgoing exterior identification and daring people to come and find them. Here are five secret restaurants that have developed such a following that they have persisted for decades in many cases, attracting crowds with good solid food delivered in total obscurity.

Stand on Bedford Street in Greenwich Village, and chances are someone will come up to you and ask, "Where's **Chumley's**?" Founded in 1928, this former speakeasy is located through an unmarked door at 86 Bedford Street. It serves acceptable pub fare, mainly to college students, tourists, and slumming professionals. Real aficionados, eschewing the food in favor of the superb selection of microbrews in the bar, refuse to enter at 86 Bedford, preferring the even more discrete entrance around the corner and through the courtyard at 58 Barrow Street, known as Pamela Court — a name that also doesn't appear anywhere.

To get to **Nick's Place** (550 Seventh Avenue, 221-3294), enter the loading dock directly to the right of 205 West 39th Street, walk past the freight elevators and continue a short way down a hallway with yellow walls. A quick left and you're in the restaurant — an enclosure painted two shades of institutional green that might once have been a mail room or a shipping office. Nick's is nominally a Greek joint, offering a few Hellenic standards like spinach pie and moussaka. But the denizens of this neighborhood, known as "garmentos" because they work in the garment center, come here for the entree salads, which are served in giant plastic bowls and cost from $3 to $7. Also fab is the feta cheeseburger. With no sign whatever, inside or outside, Nick's has lingered right off the loading dock for 24 years.

Perched on a narrow balcony high above the floor of the National Jewelers Exchange, and accessible by two narrow stairways in the rear corners, is **Diamond Dairy Restaurant** (4 West 47th Street, mezzanine, 719-2694). There is nothing to identify this place as a

restaurant except the sight of waitresses hurrying to and fro overhead with heaping plates. Grab one of the tables next to the
windows and enjoy the free show down below on the trading floor
as diamonds and antique jewelry change hands. The cuisine is kosher
dairy, which precludes any dish containing meat or chicken. Fish is
permitted. The style of the food dates from a time when overboiled
vegetables and big bowls of sour cream were considered health food.
One of the best things to order is cholent and kugel, a big plate of
rich stew containing barley and large white beans, flavored with lots
of garlic and black pepper. In the middle shines a plank of bright
orange kugel, dense and fibrous, which seems to be made of sweet
potato, but is not.

The **Arthur Avenue Retail Market** in the Belmont section of the
Bronx is one of the last operating covered markets in the city. It was
built by Fiorello LaGuardia in 1940 to get the pushcarts off the street
(see Secret Markets). Stalls sell meat, cheese, fruits and vegetables,
gardening supplies, dry pasta, coffee, and olives. Most products are
unmistakably Italian; if you have any doubts, look up and see row
upon row of small Italian flags under the lofty ceiling. Against the
rear wall of the market is **Café al Mercato** (2344 Arthur Avenue,
Bronx, 718-719-2694), with a seating area separated from the rest
of the market by a low, faux-brick wall, upon which sit wood replicas
of the Niña, Pinta, and Santa Maria. Displayed in glass cases in a
manner calculated to induce instant hunger are rice balls, crusty
loaves of bread, roasted peppers, stuffed shells, and several rectan-
gular pizzas, available by the slice. If you're sliced out, try the
frittata, a crustless pie of eggs and vegetables cooked in the pizza
oven. On a recent Saturday, every table at the café was taken by
shoppers loaded down with packages. Pretty good for a joint with
no sign on the street.

The above establishments passively keep you out by not providing signs and concealing themselves. But what about a restaurant that actively discourages you from entering it? **Katsuhama** (11 East 47th Street, 758-5909) is a Japanese café that specializes in very lean pork cutlets breaded and quickly fried. Pretty narrow specialty, eh? They know that you won't appreciate such subtlety, hence an employee is posted by the front door to dissuade you from entering. You must persevere! Katsuhama is secreted directly behind a prefab sushi bar, and a rather unpromising one at that, with the sushi already made and arranged in little Styrofoam trays. Proceed past the sushi bar and through a curtain, and approach St. Peter with a recitation you should rehearse in advance: "Yes, I know that this place serves only pork cutlets and not sushi." It helps to say "tonkatsu-ya," the Japanese term for this sort of restaurant. Once inside, you'll find what all the fuss is about.

SECRET

HI-FI

❊

The rush to dominance of the coldhearted CD rendered on digital equipment has made many nostalgic for the warm and human tones — scratches and all — of a record spun on tube-driven equipment. A couple of places in town exist to fulfill such retro-sound fantasies. **Sound by Singer** (18 East 16th Street, 924-8600) specializes in tube amps, which exude unearthly green or orange glows and top out, pricewise, at $27,000 (although cheaper models are available at less than $1,000). **Tubesville** (153 Ludlow Street, 529-7345) custom builds guitar amps as well as home stereos and will rebuild sound equipment that has been unearthed in flea markets — these markets are an easy and cheap source of such components (see Secret Flea Markets).

SECRET HOLOCAUST

Once Washington DC had its own Holocaust Museum, we had to have one too. The **Museum of the Jewish Heritage** (18 First Place, Battery Park City, 968-1800, Web site: www.mjhnyc.org) occupies a distinguished new building in a splendid garden location right on the Hudson River. Shaped like a Mesopotamian ziggurat, the museum consists of three floors connected by some really weird escalators. Wisely, the emphasis is on an upbeat presentation of Jewish life and culture, although the second, Holocaust floor deals a powerful punch. But instead of Washington's mournful room full of shoes, there's a tribute to 2,000 French-Jewish Auschwitz deportees who are represented by normal family photographs that show them at their best rather than their most abject. A spiral notebook tells their stories, providing as much information as could be recovered.

My favorite exhibit is a video showing examples of synagogue architecture from Cochin, India, to Corsicana, Texas, and my only complaint about the museum is that it overemphasizes European Jews at the expense of African, Middle Eastern, and Asian.

S E C R E T
HOT DOGS
⚜

There's no cheaper lunch than a pair of dogs snagged at **Gray's Papaya** (402 Sixth Avenue, 260-3532). The frankfurters are crisp-skinned — they pop when you bite into them — and the flesh is deep red and flavorful. Unbelievably priced at two for a dollar, they can be topped with any combo of sauerkraut, caramelized onions, ketchup, and mustard, and wrapped to go or served at the stainless-steel counter, which affords wonderful views of 8th Street and Sixth Avenue, an important Greenwich Village crossroads. No other food is available at this monomaniacal joint, which seems to have been transported from another era (when hot dogs were considered health food, or at least good food), and the only beverages offered are decanted from a line of gleaming cylindrical reservoirs that contain watery and gritty fruit beverages like papaya, pineapple, coconut, and orange. I guess the beverages are part of the whole strange experience, but I prefer to grab a soda at the convenience mart across the street.

Similar establishments flourish in other parts of town, in particular **Papaya King** (179 East 86th Street, 369-0648) on the Upper East Side and **Gray's Papaya** (2090 Broadway, 799-0243) on the Upper West Side. Unfortunately, the weenies are $1.29 each at the former, with a similar selection of beverages. Papaya King is actually listed in the *Zagat Survey*, though it claims that a meal there will cost you $9. Who in their right mind would eat so many hot dogs?

Great hot dogs with similar properties are also to be had at the city's Jewish delis, in particular **Katz's** (205 East Houston Street, 254-2246). Of course, the father of all dogs is to be found at Coney

Island's weenie palace, **Nathan's** (Surf and Stillwell Avenues, across from the subway station), founded by Nathan Handwerker, one of the original purveyors of these tube steaks on the Coney Island boardwalk. Handwerker was among a handful of salesmen who first introduced this German sausage into the United States; it remained for a sportswriter to dub them hot dogs after noting at a baseball game their resemblance to dachshunds. The crinkle-cut fries at Nathan's make a perfect accompaniment to the dogs.

Note that all the foregoing examples are browned on a griddle prior to serving. An army of **street vendors** also hawks decent dogs from carts all over town, priced at an average of $1. These are tasty, but are unfortunately warmed in boiling water, making them rather anemic in texture and flavor. They're known disdainfully by frank aficionados as "floaters" — a term borrowed from coroners, who apply it to corpses found floating in the river.

SECRET

ICE CREAM

❧

If you want to sample the Big Apple's best ice cream, you're going to have to get more specific. For creamy, Midwestern-style ice cream, I'd pick **Chinatown Ice Cream Factory** (65 Bayard Street, 608-4170), where the product is light and sweet and obviously fresh-made. A plus for the adventuresome are some of the Asian flavors, like coconut, lichee, green tea, mango, and red bean — although the usual flavors are also well represented and well worth sampling. Other parlors for "normal" ice cream in a ice-cream-parlor ambiance include **Eggers** (1194 Forest Avenue, Staten Island, 718-981-2110),

Peter's (185 Atlantic Avenue, Brooklyn, 718-852-3835), and, best of all, **Eddie's Sweet Shop** (105-29 Metropolitan Avenue, Forest Hills, Queens, 718-520-8514).

For ice cream with a Caribbean flair, check out **Taste of the Tropics** (1839 Nostrand Avenue, Brooklyn, 718-856-0821). This Flatbush ice-cream factory specializes in exotic tropical flavors: soursop, coconut, grapefruit, mango, papaya, rum and raisin, and Guinness stout, if it's not too early in the day for you. All the usual flavors are also available, and the product is rich and creamy.

If you want real old-fashioned frozen custard, which derives its richness from egg yolks as well as heavy cream, **Custard Beach** (World Financial Center, 225 Liberty Street, 786-4707) is your place. The standard flavors are vanilla and chocolate, and they scoop an additional wild-card flavor each day, like maple nut, coffee, or pistachio. The frozen custard rivals those I've tasted across Wisconsin, the national home of custard. Vanilla is the best way to encounter this rich treat.

But mere ice cream or frozen custard will always be second in the hearts of New Yorkers to Italian ices, available more universally than ice cream — from every corner bodega and pushcart, both Hispanic and Italian. A couple of places qualify as Italian ice royalty. The **Lemon Ice King of Corona** (52–02 108th Street, Corona, Queens, 718-699-5133) isn't kidding — the eponymous flavor is properly tart, laced with fine shreds of lemon rind that add an extra dimension. It's one of the city's most perfect foods. The other 49 or so flavors are also estimable, including my surprise favorite, watermelon, which has a few seeds in it for authenticity. Other folks swear the best ices are found at **Ciao Bella**, a much more modern establishment that supplies custom ice creams and ices to the fanciest restaurants in town. I like to patronize the retail window at their manufacturing facility (262 Mott Street, 226-7668), but the other two locations may be more convenient for you (27 East 92nd Street, 831-5555; 200 West 57th Street, 956-5555). Other places with good but not excellent ices sometimes distinguish themselves with a single exceptional variety: the venerable **Veniero's** (342 East 11th Street, 674-4415) in the East Village peddles a cantaloupe ice made from pureed fruit at the height of ripeness, while **Bleecker Street Pastry** (245 Bleecker Street, 242-4959) is famous for its apricot ice, with coconut a close second.

SECRET

INDIAN

❖

There are several Indian neighborhoods in New York City. The most famous is the worst — the block of **East 6th Street between First and Second Avenues**, where an astonishing collection of dim, low-priced restaurants sling stewed meats in midnight gravies. It used to be said that the curries were piped underground from a central source to these 20-odd places, and there is actually some truth to that statement: the proprietors of nearly all came from a single town in Bangladesh and generally had little cooking experience before emigrating here. Nevertheless, a walk down the street is filled with pungent smells and visual diversion, and you can enjoy the sitar and tabla players furiously strumming and drumming in the windows from outside the restaurants. One or two of these places may sometimes serve up a satisfying meal, but I leave it to you to find out which. There are also a couple of worthy Indian groceries around the corner on First Avenue that sell spices in bulk at shockingly low prices.

Much more righteous is the stretch of **Lexington Avenue between 25th and 29th Streets**, waggishly known as **Curry Hill** (Murray Hill is the official name of the district). This neighborhood abounds in restaurants, sari showrooms, newsagents, and spice stores that cater to Indians from all over the city, although few live in the vicinity anymore. The menus in the cafés are evenly divided between vegetarian and nonvegetarian fare, and they reflect the religious and dining preferences of all Indians. In this tiny neighborhood, Sikhs, Muslims, Hindus, and Jains all coexist peacefully as they pursue the almighty dollar.

This strip of Lexington is also a great place to pick up a cheap meal — although there are more expensive restaurants, too. **Curry in a Hurry** (119 Lexington Avenue, 683-0904) makes South Indian vegetarian eats like masala dosai and utthapam to order in the front window, in addition to Mughal vegetarian and nonvegetarian fare. Cheaper still is **East in the West** (113 Lexington Avenue, 683-1313), where a vegetarian combination consisting of basmati rice, three choices from the steam table, salad, chutney, raita, and a poofy nan fresh from the oven may be had for only $5.

But for the real Indianophile, a pilgrimage to **Jackson Heights** is obligatory. Like Curry Hill, this commercial strip attracts subcontinentals from all over the borough of Queens. It's where you go to buy a sari at one of a half-dozen boutiques, acquire compatible video equipment to ship back home to your family in Madras, shop for vegetables and fruits unknown to Westerners, and scarf some of the best Indian food in town at **Jackson Diner** (37–47 74th Street, 718-672-1232), which recently moved from its cramped, pink-walled location down the street (once a Greek diner, hence the name) into luxurious new digs. The $5.99 all-you-can-eat luncheon buffet is still one of the best deals in town, and the food is more subtly and complexly spiced than it is for the same price anywhere else.

On the same block, **Butala Emporium** (37–46 74th Street, 718-899-5590) provides the city's best selection of Indian books, including dictionaries in Hindi, Bengali, Urdu, and Sanskrit, and the latest publications in an even greater variety of languages. There, too, you'll find cookbooks, drums, carom sets, ayurvedic medicines, and, for $325, a magnificent hanging metalwork temple that would look great in any apartment. Around the corner, at 37th Avenue and 73rd Street, you'll find three Indian greengrocers that stock a broad range of inexpensive Indian produce, the odder of which are actually now grown in the United States, mainly in Florida: fresh fenugreek leaves, yard beans (so called because these green beans are nearly a yard long), kareli (a wrinkled gourd), and muli (a long white radish). Henna tattoos are a specialty of **Menka Beauty Salon** (37–56 74th Street, 718-424-6851).

There's a magnificent **Hindu temple** (45–57 Bowne Street, Queens) in nearby Flushing, a three-towered structure honoring Ganesh, tethered to the ground with tiny lights as if it might sail heavenward. Next door is **Dosa Hutt** (45–63 Bowne Street, 718-961-5897), a small lunch counter that serves the best dosa in the city — potato-stuffed crepes that are the soul of South Indian cooking.

SECRET

JAPANESE

✢

A Japanese friend told me there are three fan magazines published in Tokyo that concentrate exclusively on New York's East Village. This bohemian neighborhood has become home to thousands of young Japanese expatriates who dress in wonderfully outlandish styles while retaining a good deal of native charm and humility. Many are artists and musicians. The epicenter of this scene is **the intersection of 9th and Stuyvesant Streets**, an area that may in the future become known as **Little Tokyo**. There are, of course, several good Japanese restaurants here, but a better place to dig the scene is **Sunrise Mart** (4 Stuyvesant Street, 598-3040), a supermarket carrying every Nipponese product imaginable: fresh fish, frozen dumplings, shaved beef for sukiyaki, imported beers, bottled sauces, unusual vegetables, CDs, novelty candies, liquid vitamin supplements, and mayonnaise (a Japanese obsession) in cute little kewpie-doll squeeze bottles. In short, the store presents a primer on Japanese culture. There's also a take-out food display in the rear where you can get wacky kimchee omelets, decent sushi and sashimi, and plain boiled rice.

Down the block is **Decibel** (240 East 9th Street, 979-2733), a subterranean bar with one of the city's best sake selections; it's especially hopping after midnight. **Angel's Share** (you figure out what it means — 8 Stuyvesant Street, 777-5415) is an excellent tavern with a commanding view of the one of the East Village's busiest squares, which has recently been spruced up with a municipally maintained garden. Angel's Share is part of a complex called **Yokucho Village**, also home to a restaurant specializing in the Japanese version of Korean barbecue, a central café decorated like a village and offering small meals (including most of the things routinely designated appetizers on Japanese menus). Bargain-priced noodles are to be found at the elegant **Soba-ya** (229 East 9th Street, 533-6966).

While the bohos hang in the East Village, more well-heeled Japanese business people prefer the area of Midtown bounded by Fifth and

Madison Avenues, and 44th and 50th Streets. Wander along any of these blocks and discover fancy restaurants serving the many varieties of Japanese cuisine. **Naniwa** (4 East 46th Street, 370-4045), for example, will serve you a complete four-course dinner of fugu, the fish tainted with a poison that's 1,000 times more toxic than cyanide, until rendered harmless by a chef licensed by the government of Japan. (Ask to see the certificate — it's in the cloak closet.) You won't find this important restaurant in the *Zagat Survey*, since it's patronized almost exclusively by a Japanese clientele. Across the street is **Genki** (9 East 46th Street, 983-5018), a sushi bar that sends its small dishes around the room on a conveyor belt from which you make your selection, and often has spectacular specials, like nigiri-zushi made from belly tuna flown in from Chile.

But if you want to go completely Japanese, make the short hop across the Hudson River to Edgewater, New Jersey, where you'll find **Yaohan Plaza** (595 River Road, 201-941-9113). This all-Japanese mall boasts a football-field-sized supermarket, food court, full-service restaurant perched on the edge of the river, and home furnishings and electronics stores. The selection at the supermarket in the fresh-fish aisles is not to be believed, but perhaps more interesting are the American products the store chooses to stock. Subsidized buses leave regularly from the **Port Authority Bus Terminal** at 41st Street and Eighth Avenue in Manhattan. Call 564-8484 for the schedule.

For a dose of high culture, try the **Japan Society** (333 East 47th Street, 752-0824), which mounts art exhibitions, offers language classes, and screens a distinguished film program. Performers and lecturers from Japan are also presented in the auditorium, and there's a library stocked with the latest Japanese periodicals. All activities are open to nonmembers for a nominal charge. Speaking of periodicals, the largest selection of Japanese magazines in the city is to be found at the huge bookstore, **Asahiya** (52 Vanderbilt Avenue, 883-0011), right across the street from Grand Central Station. This establishment also carries tons of English-language books about Japan, Japanese bestsellers translated into English, and collateral items like origami sets, *Hello Kitty* comics, and cookbooks. Be warned that 95% of the material is in Japanese.

SECRET

KARAOKE

❧

The bizarre practice of karaoke, popular across the US 10 years ago, is staging a surprising comeback in downtown New York among wise-guy scenesters. The premier spot is the **Lansky Lounge** (104 Norfolk Street, 677-9489), the back-room restaurant and cocktail lounge of the staid Jewish dairy restaurant **Ratner's** The *Times* recently reported that the Wednesday-night event has been attracting celebrities like Ben Affleck and Mark Wahlberg (no, that wasn't his real schlong you saw in *Boogie Nights*). A related venue for karaoke is the **Elbow Room** (144 Bleecker Street, 979-8434), where the show starts at 11 P.M. on Wednesday nights and runs till 4 A.M. Guests crooning in synch with the big video screen have included Michael Stipe, Moby, and Elliot Smith. Another hipster location is **Village Karaoke** (27 Cooper Square, 254-0066), which features a series of private rooms where you can indulge in secret; choose lyrics in Japanese, Korean, Chinese, or English.

At the foregoing establishments, patrons are likely to sing off-key intentionally and generally cut up, so if you're serious about your karaoke you may want to seek out one of the more traditional bars that offer it in **Koreatown** (32nd through 36th Streets, between Broadway and Fifth Avenue) or in Manhattan's **Chinatown**; look for the signs posted out front. **Winnie's** (104 Bayard Street, 962-8393) is one of Chinatown's more prominent bars, offering karaoke seven nights a week, and you ain't heard nothin' till you've heard "Proud Mary" sung there in Chinese. Further afield, there's **Rhodes** (City Island Avenue, Bronx, 718-885-1538) on City Island, the seafood and yachting capital of the Bronx, where Saturday night is karaoke night. Or you can also sing yourself blue at **Kim Yung** (181–08 Union Turnpike, 718-380-1918), a Chinese-Polynesian restaurant in Flushing, Queens, on Wednesday and Friday nights.

S E C R E T

KIDS

✧

Most of the activities suggested in this book are suitable for children, but here are a few places that will especially appeal to the younger set.

There are many children's museums in the metropolitan area, including the **Children's Museum of the Arts** (72 Spring Street, 274-0986), providing lots of hands-on arts activities; the **Children's Museum of Manhattan** (212 West 83rd Street, 721-1234), offering a decidedly effete Upper West Side view of childhood; **Staten Island Children's Museum** (Snug Harbor Cultural Center, 1000 Richmond Terrace, Staten Island, 718-273-2060), an institution with an ecological bent located adjacent to a botanical garden in a former sailors' retirement home a short, scenic shuttle ride

from the Staten Island Ferry; **Liberty Science Center** (Liberty State Park, 201-200-1000), New Jersey's state-of-the-art science museum, which provides the little ones with plenty of stuff to do but is way too crowded; and, also in a technological vein, **New York Hall of Science** (Flushing Meadows Park, Queens, 718-699-0005), a recently refurbished and charming relic of the 1964–65 World's Fair, easily combined with a visit to nearby **Shea Stadium** for a Mets game. But best of all is the **Brooklyn Children's Museum** (145 Brooklyn Avenue, 718-735-4400), situated underground and approached via a mysterious tunnel. Founded in 1899, it was the first children's museum in the country.

Kids will also dig the *Forbes Magazine* **Gallery and Museum of the City of New York** (see Secret Obscure Museums), as well as the **American Museum of Natural History** (79th Street and Central Park West, 769-5100), first in the nation in dinosaur acquisitions, and impossible to navigate during peak hours. The **New York Doll Hospital** (787 Lexington Avenue, 838-7527) is a cluttered Victorian triage center for dolls where you may purchase dolls as well as have them fixed. No kid will want to miss FAO **Schwartz** (767 Fifth Avenue, 644-9410), an immense and expensive toy showroom that manages to get new toy crazes months before its chain-store counterparts, or **Game Show** (1240 Lexington Avenue, 472-8011; and 474 Sixth Avenue, 633-6328), an emporium that offers many brainy options for young puzzlers and gamesters.

The ornate and bargain-priced **carousel in Central Park** (64th Street mid-park), boasting immense hand-carved horses in the "Coney Island" style, is still thrilling. Walk away from it in any direction and you'll encounter elaborate playgrounds and climbable rock formations that will delight children. The small-scale and elaborately landscaped **Central Park Zoo** (Fifth Avenue and 64th

Street, 861-6030) is, for me, the best in the city, notable for its indoor rainforest, penguin house, and outdoor polar-bear environment.

One of the best restaurants for children is the **Cowgirl Hall of Fame** (519 Hudson Street, 633-1133), serving up comfort food and white-trash cooking in a series of dining rooms rife with ranch memorabilia, including the periodically changing exhibit celebrating rodeo cowgirls that gives the facility a quasi-feminist edge. **Chinatown** is also a favorite kids' eating locale (see Secret Chinatown), especially the dim-sum parlors like **Golden Unicorn** (18 East Broadway, 941-0911), where dumplings and other small snacks are wheeled by on carts from 9 A.M. till mid-afternoon. Finally, the name alone attracts youngsters to the **Lexington Candy Shop Luncheonette** (1226 Lexington Avenue, 288-0057), a joint with a '40s decor featuring swiveling stools and Naugahyde banquets, with real soda jets (see Secret Egg Creams) and a plain and kid-friendly menu of burgers, eggs, malts, and sandwiches.

If you want to be a hero to your offspring, take them to **Lazer Park** (163 West 46th Street, 398-3060), a laser-tag facility deep below Times Square; or the **Sony** IMAX theater (1998 Broadway, 336-5000), where you get to wear a big machine on your face to watch blessedly short features on a screen they claim is the largest in the world.

S E C R E T
KITES
✤

If somebody tells you to "go fly a kite," oblige them. My personal search for these devices began at **Toys 'R Us** at Herald Square (Sixth Avenue and 33rd Street), where I figured I'd get the best selection at the lowest price. Nope! The lumbering chain stores don't bother carrying kites — one of the most ancient, reliable, and desirable toys on Earth — because they're not manufactured and promoted by the big toy manufacturers. Luckily, New York has **Big City Kite Company** (1210 Lexington Avenue, 472-2623). Here the average kite will cost you $25 (and some go for as little as $15), though you can pay over $100 for competition models. All accessories are available. The kites are manufactured in China, Japan, India, and here in the United States; some are even attractive enough to hang on your walls.

New York is one of the windiest cities in the country (even windier, on average, than Chicago, the Windy City), so you won't have any trouble getting your new purchase aloft. It is difficult, however, to find enough room to fly it. Central Park provides the best opportunities, especially the **Sheep Meadow** (enter at West 62nd Street) or the **Great Lawn** (enter at West 81st Street), where a good deal of the city's kite action occurs. **East River Park** (enter at 10th Street, 6th Street, or Houston) is also a good bet, as are **Inwood Hill Park** (approached via the 207th Street stop on the A train) and the **North Meadow** at Battery Park City (enter at Chambers Street). Brooklyn's **Prospect Park** and Queens's **Flushing Meadows-Corona Park** are favorite spots as well.

SECRET
LESBIANS

❧

Though gay men's nightspots have migrated northward into Chelsea and Hell's Kitchen, Greenwich Village remains the hotbed of lesbian culture. Sisters can be seen strutting proudly up and down Hudson

Street, and some of their favorite institutions include **Henrietta Hudson** (448 Hudson Street, 924-3347), a homey neighborhood bar where a prominent talk-show host can be seen hanging out some evenings, and **Nanny's** (21 Seventh Avenue South, 366-6312), preferred by a slightly younger and more glamorous crowd. Greenwich Village also has its own lesbian restaurant, **Rubyfruit Bar and Grill** (531 Hudson Street, 929-3343), with a menu of solid American fare featuring big hunks of meat and fish, and a hopping upstairs bar enjoyed by a broad spectrum of patrons, from femmes to diesel dykes. If you prefer the artsier East Village scene complete with live music and other types of performance, check out **Meow Mix** (269 East Houston Street, 254-1434), mainly for women, but also open to men. **Wonder Bar** (505 East Sixth Street, 777-9105) has live DJs, and is especially mobbed on weekends.

In Brooklyn, there's a lesbian scene happening in Park Slope that rivals that of Greenwich Village. It's centered on **Rising Café** (186 Fifth Avenue, 718-622-5072), a convivial coffee house, and **Carry Nation** (363 Fifth Avenue, 718-788-0924), the pioneering bar in the area. Nightclub action is found at **Sanctuary** (44 Seventh Avenue, 718-832-9800). For further clues, consult **Shades of Lavender** (470 Bergen Street, 718-622-2910), an organization housed in the same neighborhood that provides support services and organizes social events.

Information central for the citywide community is the **Lesbian Switchboard** (741-2610), an all-volunteer organization that provides listings and referral services. **Eve's Garden** (119 West 57th Street, suite 1201, 757-8651) is an erotic boutique that caters exclusively to women and their same-sex partners; stocking sex toys, videos, and print material, it's probably the only store of its kind in the country. And the Eve's Garden bulletin board is a clearinghouse

of contacts and events. Finally, there's **Women's One World**, or
wow (59 East 4th Street, 777-4280), a wildly experimental and
coalition-building theater group that holds regular strategy meetings
open to all women.

S E C R E T

LIBRARIES

❧

Any branch of the **New York Public Library** is open to the public
— and that includes outlanders as well as city residents. You don't
need a card to use the collections or just snooze in a chair. If you
want to get a library card you can get one on the spot, but you've
got to present a minimal proof of address, like a bill with a New
York address on it. Accordingly, if you don't really live here, file
a change of address for some credit-card bill (or, even better, a
collection-agency notice), and have it sent to an address in New York
City where you can retrieve it.

But the majority of library materials are held for reference and
don't circulate anyway, so you don't really need a card. Many of the
neighborhood branch libraries are architecturally distinguished, like
the **Jefferson Market Branch** (425 Sixth Avenue, 243-4334), an
ancient courthouse with a spooky bell tower approached via a
twisting stairway à la Hitchcock's *Vertigo*; the **Ottendorfer Branch**
(135 Second Avenue, 674-0947), originally a German-language
library donated by a pair of wealthy philanthropists (you can
still make out the slogan "Freie Bibliothek Und Lesehalle" on the
lintel); and the **Aguilar Branch** (174 East 110th Street, 535-2930),

a handsome three-story structure, framed by towering classical columns, originally founded in 1886 as a Jewish lending library and named for an English-Sephardic author, Grace Aguilar.

Some branch libraries specialize, and the results are spectacular. Take the Lincoln Center's **Performing Arts Library** (40 Lincoln Center, 870-1600), an extensive collection of dance, theater, and orchestra materials where exhibitions of theater playbills and other ephemera are often presented. A former department store was recently converted into the new **Science-Industry and Business Library** (188 Madison Avenue, 592-7000), a collection indispensable to anyone doing business research or job hunting in these sectors. Harlem's **Schomburg Center** (515 Malcolm X Boulevard, 491-2200) is a research library specializing in African-American history with an international reputation in the field.

But the most visit-worthy establishment is still the main branch of the **New York Public Library** (455 Fifth Avenue, 661-7220), the one with the stone lions out front. The magnificent Main Reading Room has just been restored to its 1911 grandeur, with arched windows and a carved wooden ceiling featuring cherubs and satyrs with a painted-cloud mortise that makes you feel like you're in heaven. There are 125 miles of stacks, and, reputedly, rollerblading clerks retrieve the books. The new room has hookups for laptops that allow you to tap directly into the catalog. Anyone may order a book and use it within the confines of the reading room — none of the materials circulates.

SECRET
LINGERIE

❖

With their catalogs landing in every mailbox in the country, **Victoria's Secret** has become old hat. Nevertheless, they have stores at 34 East 57th Street (758-5592) and 115 Fifth Avenue (477-4118) if you want to inspect before you purchase or browse for sale bargains. But for more unique creations, check out **Samantha Jones** (996 Lexington Avenue, 628-7720), which specializes in up-to-the-minute colors and skimpy styles; and **La Petite Coquette** (51 University Place, 473-2478), stocked with plenty of designs imported from Italy and France; this store's window displays often provoke blushes, highly unusual in Greenwich Village. An establishment called AM/PM (109 Thompson Street, 219-0343) features bustiers and other wonders of undergarment architecture, while **Bra Smyth** (905 Madison Avenue, 772-9400) custom builds brassieres for hard-to-fit shapes. **La Perla** (777 Madison Avenue, 459-2775) is lauded for its helpful sales staff. Everything here is manufactured to the company's specifications, including generous as well as skimpy styles; the downside: premium price.

SECRET
LITERARY SCENE

❖

Since 1994, KGB (85 East 4th Street, 505-3360) has been the center of the East Village's thriving literary scene. Historically a leftist meeting hall, it's been transformed into a Soviet-themed bar and writer's hangout. Devotees include literary lights Aimee Bender,

Rick Moody, and Luc Sante; the latter's epic history *Low Life* chronicles the seamy underworld of New York City from 1840 to 1920, peering into opium dens, gambling houses, and vice scenes of every sort, an antidote to the official histories of the city. Many evenings, KGB features free readings, including one on the third Tuesday of every month sponsored by *Granta* magazine; keep your eye on the *Voice*, *Time Out*, and other publications (see Secret Periodicals) for announcements. An anthology called *The KGB Bar Reader* was published late in 1998 by William Morrow.

For a strikingly different ambiance, check out the **Nuyorican Poets Café** (236 East 3rd Street, 505-8183), home of the poetry slam, a curious genre wherein poets compete in an almost athletic fashion and are judged by a panel and awarded prizes. Far more sedate are the readings at **Three Lives & Company** (154 West 10th Street, 741-2069), a charming, author-oriented bookstore in the West Village that recently presented a reading by actor and playwright Wallace Shawn, and the **92nd Street Y** (1395 Lexington Avenue, 996-1100), where a hefty admission is charged and the high-powered program includes literati such as Tom Wolfe, David Mamet, and Alice Walker.

Of course, chain bookstores like **Barnes & Noble**, **Borders**, and **Rizzoli** host armies of touring authors flogging their books. Barnes & Noble, headquartered in New York, conducts the most aggressive program at its recently created megastores, which some fear are driving the neighborhood and specialty bookshops out of business. At any rate, the megastores are always plastered with placards advertising these literary gigs. Recent readers at the Union Square branch include Eric Bogosian and Joyce Carol Oates.

Verse lovers pick up the free monthly *Poetry Calendar* (611 Broadway, suite 905, 260-7097, Web site: www.poets.org), which, in addition to day-by-day listings of readings, also notes radio broadcasts, submission calls for other publications, essays on poetry, and poems by writers, famous and not. Many events are free; few are more than $5.

Or just hang out at a bar with a rich literary history, like the **White Horse** or **Cedar Tavern** (see Secret Bars).

SECRET

LONDON BUS TOURS

A few years ago fleets of double-decker buses hit the streets — actually imported from London. Three companies offer rides on these lumbering behemoths, which follow looped routes through Midtown, Downtown, and Harlem. Usually, you pay by the day, and one ticket allows you to board and reboard as often as you want. Stops are located at obvious places like the Metropolitan Museum and the World Trade Center. From the upper deck, at least, you get an imperial view of some of the busiest parts of the city — occasionally, when you're stuck in traffic, a much longer view than you need. Another drawback is the bitter gaze of the locals, who resent these buses jammed with tourists who don't want — the residents fantasize — to sully themselves walking the streets. Still, kids love these buses, and they're also a boon to the elderly and the footsore.

Gray Line Tours (397-2600) depart from the Port Authority Bus Terminal at 42nd Street and Eighth Avenue. They offer a number of options in the $20-to-$30 range, with buses departing every 20 or 30 minutes depending on which of the three interconnecting routes is to be followed. **New York Apple Tours** (944-9200) offers a more comprehensive single route in Manhattan, which goes from 125th

Street in Harlem down to the Battery at Manhattan's southernmost tip; the all-day option is priced at $35. A second day is offered for free. As a bonus, you can use this pass to board a bus that does Brooklyn, or at least some of the nearer parts of it, beginning at Battery Park. The Manhattan routes commence at 41st Street and Seventh Avenue, although you can arrange to board the bus en route. **New York Double Decker Tours** (967-6008) depart from the Empire State Building at 34th Street and Fifth Avenue. Their uptown and downtown routes interconnect, and the fare is also $35 per day. Buses run every 20 minutes till 10 P.M., and a second, free day can be used anytime within the next 10 days.

Despite the appeal of these buses, touring by subway is much faster and cheaper, especially when combined with a walking tour or two (see Secret Walking Tours).

S E C R E T
MAPS
✤

Indispensable to orienteering in the city is Hagstrom's wonderful *New York City 5 Borough Atlas*, available in a 10-by-13-inch format, which divides the city into 31 contiguous maps, or the almost-pocket-sized 5-by-8-inch format, with 65 maps. Take my advice and get the larger size, or go crazy flipping between maps looking for your destination. Ignoring cosmetic considerations, I fold the large version twice to fit in a small backpack — I'm never without mine. Both versions have street indexes for every borough, list thousands of points of interest right on the maps, and include street numbers along most routes, so it's easy to locate a destination by address within a block or two. The maps are found in most bookstores (go to a Barnes & Noble or B. Dalton to be certain), and sell for $10.95 (big format) and $8.95 (little).

Also indispensable is a subway map, the new version of which has a five-borough map with bus linkages and other transit linkages on one side and on the other an area map showing commuter rail lines that travel far into Connecticut, Long Island, and New Jersey. You can pick one up for free at any subway token booth.

Two stores specialize in maps from all over the world: **Hagstrom Map & Travel Center** (57 West 43rd Street, 398-1222) and **Rand McNally** (150 East 52nd Street, 758-7488). Armchair travelers will also delight in the **Complete Traveller** (199 Madison Avenue, 685-9007), which, in addition to maps, boasts the most complete collection of travel guides in the city and has an entire room devoted to out-of-print travel books.

If you collect antique maps, the best source is **Argosy Book Store** (116 East 59th Street, 753-4455), where the maps are organized by year of origin and some are hundreds of years old. **Pageant Book and Print Shop** (114 West Houston Street, 674-5296) has nearly as many old maps, but in a more anarchistic order and with correspondingly lower prices.

SECRET
MARKETS

❖

In the early part of the twentieth century, most city dwellers did their shopping from pushcarts that hawked fish, vegetables, hardware, apparel, and every other conceivable item that could be pushed in a wheeled conveyance. These carts would often congregate at street corners and wide spots in the road, like Gansevoort Street in Greenwich Village and Orchard Street on the Lower East Side. Sure, they congested the thoroughfares, but who cared? Then as automobile traffic increased, campaigns were undertaken to disperse the welter of carts. Prime orchestrator was Mayor Fiorella LaGuardia, who inaugurated a citywide system of covered markets in the '40s, although most of the vendors complained that the cost of operating a stall was too great.

Few of the LaGuardia markets still exist. The best preserved is the **Arthur Avenue Retail Market** (2344 Arthur Avenue) in the Belmont section of the Bronx. The products sold here are mainly Italian, and it's an especially great place to buy fresh handmade cheeses like mozzarella and ricotta, and cured meats like prosciutto di Parma and the unbelievably funky air-dried sausage called soppressata, available in sweet and hot versions. The market itself is exhilarating. As you watch customers carefully picking over the offerings and kibitzing with vendors you're likely to regret how much of the marketing experience has been lost in today's sterile supermarkets. An excellent lunch counter, **Café al Mercato** (718-364-7681), is located in the rear, and make sure to stroll up and down Arthur Avenue and admire this retrograde Italian enclave.

In Manhattan, one third of the Lower East Side's **Essex Street Retail Market** has been revived — the block between Delancey and Rivington on the east side of the street. Reflecting the current ethnic character of the neighborhood, most of the vendors purvey products with a Latin tinge. Thus the vegetable vendors specialize in starchy roots like yuca, apro, nawe, and tautia. At the three butcher stalls, you'll find oxtails, hog maws, and trotters. A vestige of what was once a mainly Jewish neighborhood, a kosher seafood counter, sells no shellfish or squid, but has a pristine display of many kinds of fish, including humongous tilefish cut in half to reveal yellow sacks of roe. There's also a bicycle-repair stall that sells used bikes and roller blades, and a number of off-price clothiers. A couple blocks to the southwest, in Sara Roosevelt Park at Grand and Forsyth, is **Dragon Gate Market** an open-air Chinese market that is always on the verge of expanding and that has many food vendors, including one of the few in town selling Indonesian fare.

Another Latin-tinged covered market is **La Marqueta** (enter at 115th and Park Avenue) in East Harlem. One store specializes in bacalao; the salt cod has been a staple food of the poor in the Caribbean and southern Europe for the last few centuries. Another specializes in fancy lace and trimming for home seamstresses (and seamsters too, I suppose). A visit to this market is less exciting than a visit to those mentioned above, unless you link it with a trip to the immense, open-air **African market** a couple of blocks to the west on 116th Street (see Secret African). Your route will lie along a street that boasts more botanicas — stores selling the implements of santeria — than any other part of town. Thrill to the statues of weeping saints, love charms and potions, and strange herbs and oils in profusion.

SECRET
MARTINIS

✤

I've never been sure what all the fuss is about with martinis — you're basically drinking straight vodka or gin from an appealingly angular glass. But whether you prefer yours with an olive, a twist of lemon, or a cocktail onion (technically, a Gibson), the best are to be had at **Angel's Share** (8 Stuyvesant Street, 777-5415), a weird Japanese bar tucked away in the corner of a larger restaurant that specializes in snacks and Korean barbecue. The creation of the cocktail is a complete show in itself, as the Japanese bartenders shake and sway and then pour the libation with a grand flourish. Another joint with great martinis in multiple variations is **Martini's** (810 Seventh Avenue, 767-1717), where you can also get Italian food with a Tuscan flourish, including tasty small pizzas. Hip downtown watering hole **Bar 89** (89 Mercer Street, 274-0989) is famous for its outsized martinis, while **Torch** (137 Ludlow Street, 228-5151), on the Lower East Side, garnishes theirs with a raw oyster. **First** (87 First Avenue, 674-3823), a pricey restaurant with an adventurous menu, offers the cocktail in three different sizes, including a miniature version that allows you to sample several. One is made with Tang.

SECRET

METROCARD

❖

When the metrocard was first introduced in 1997, it revolutionized public transportation in New York. Though the base fare of $1.50 remains the same, you can load up your card with any number of fares from $3 to $80, obviating the need for a pocketful of bullseye tokens. Further, for every $15 of fare added to the reusable cards, the Metropolitan Transportation Authority (MTA) grants a single bonus fare, with additional free fares prorated for amounts over $15. For example, if you put $20 on a card, one and one-third bonus fares are credited. Note that, as of this writing, tokens can still be purchased if you prefer — and they make handsome souvenirs.

Even more important, the metrocard has allowed the rider, for the first time, to transfer from subway to bus, and vice versa. As a bonus, the transfer doesn't have to be immediate — since some subway rides from remote areas can take well over an hour, the MTA has had to build in leeway time. If you board a train in Far Rockaway, for example, and ride into Manhattan, you need most of the official two-hour limit before you dip the card a second time for the free transfer to a bus. Though it's not advertised, the limit is actually two hours and 18 minutes, reputedly the amount of time it takes to ride from the end of the Staten Island line, take the ferry into Manhattan, then transfer to a bus or subway.

This 138-minute leeway can be used to save you lots of money, since you probably won't be routinely making long trips that require it for a legitimate transfer. Let's say you're staying near Times Square and want to visit Greenwich Village. You jump on one of the Seventh Avenue buses and cruise down to Sheridan Square at the corner of Christopher Street. After enjoying lunch and walking around, you jump on subway line number 1 at Sheridan Square and ride it up to Times Square. The "transfer" is free, as long as your activities in the Village, plus the bus ride, take less than 138 minutes. In other words, take a bus in one direction, and a subway in the opposite direction, and you've saved $1.50.

This method can also be used to take two bus rides, as long as the second bus is not the same bus going in the opposite direction. Many buses take perpendicular turns and head off in odd directions, so with a bus map in hand and a willingness to walk a few blocks to begin or finish a journey, you'll be able to save a fare or two each day and feel the satisfaction of making the transportation system work for you the way New Yorkers do.

To complicate matters, the MTA introduced a new metrocard option in 1998 — the unlimited fare card — which looks identical to the pay-per-ride card mentioned above. With this option, $17 buys you unlimited rides for seven days and $63 buys you unlimited rides for 30 days. To prevent people from sharing these cards, there is a minimum of 18 minutes between swipes, which can be a pain in the ass if you want to transfer to a bus or leave the subway and then reenter within that time period. The seven-day card could be a very good deal for a tourist spending an entire week in the city, assuming he or she makes more than one round trip each day. But if you want to relax, or like to walk or take a cab now and then, it would be difficult to keep up that pace for an entire week, especially in the heat of summer or dead of winter. I still prefer the pay-per-ride, which allows you to keep all your transportation options open.

A new daily unlimited Metrocard ($4) has just been launched, although it's not for sale at most subway token booths — reportedly to keep it out of the hands of city residents. The card is good for unlimited rides, but it expires at 4 a.m. the day after you buy it, so you only get 16 hours out of it if you purchase it, say, at noon. Find it, if you can, at tourist businesses and hotel desks.

S E C R E T
MIDDLE AGES

✤

You can take the high road or the low road to the Middles Ages. The high road leads to the **Cloisters** (Fort Tryon Park, a few blocks north of the 190th Street station on the A train, 923-3700), a subsidiary branch of the Metropolitan Museum of Art located in a delightful park setting near the northern tip of Manhattan. The cobbled courtyards, herb gardens, small chapels, stained glass, grotesque reliefs, and arched walkways are intended to re-create a medieval French monastery, including Romanesque and Gothic elements. In fact, many of these constituents were pillaged (well, maybe that's too strong a word) from five abandoned French monasteries by sculptor George Gray Barnard early in the century. He was bought out by John D. Rockefeller Jr., who turned the collection over to the Metropolitan and bankrolled construction of the current complex, which opened in 1938. It's elegant and creepy at the same time — the neophyte will marvel at the consistent presentation while the medievalist will be disturbed by the odd juxtapositions of art and architecture. Taken together, the surrounding Frederick Law Olmsted Jr. park and the Cloisters, which top a ridge with panoramic views, constitute one of New York's greatest sights.

Another high road to the Middle Ages, and one particularly enjoyed by children, is the rather obscure arms and armor exhibit near the rear of the main floor of the **Metropolitan Museum of Art** (82nd Street and Fifth Avenue, 535-7710). It's the type of old-fashioned exhibit that has yet to be updated with multimedia flourishes — but it's much better that way, with miles of glass cases filled with swords, daggers, maces, poleaxes, glaves, and, of course, entire suits of armor and even horse armor, all stiffly and symmetrically displayed. The medieval-art hall nearby is also nothing to sneeze at, presenting distinguished paintings, porcelains, and bronzes.

But if high culture bores you, there's a much lower road you can take to the Middle Ages: **Medieval Times**, a turreted castle that rises up out of the swamp of the Meadowlands in Lyndhurst, New Jersey. A convenient ticket office at **Times Square** (2 Times Square Plaza, 586-9096) confiscates your $33.95, which includes a round trip on

a charter bus, four-course dinner, and show that consists of jousting and other tournaments narrated by a bellicose announcer in a fake Middle English patois peppered with "thees" and "thous." The food is as wretched as you might imagine and is consumed without utensils by the cheering throngs around the arena as, according to the publicity materials, "fifty serfs and wenches scurry to fill your tankard and attend to your every need." Enduring this spectacle with the Jersey peasants who really appreciate it was how I spent one of the most surreal evenings of my life.

SECRET
MINIATURE CITY
❧

No matter how long you spend in the Big Apple, you're never going to see every neighborhood or make much sense of its sprawling land masses, mainly islands. The only way to get an intimate sense of the city's geography is to visit the **Queens Museum of Art** (New York City Building, Flushing, 718-592-2405), the former New York City Pavilion of the 1964–65 World's Fair. The greatest attraction is not the art, but a huge model of the entire city in 3-D. At a scale of one inch equals 100 feet, it's 154 feet long and 137 feet wide and has over 895,000 individual structures. Updated in 1992, the model is now squeaky clean and reasonably accurate. Tiny airplanes take off from the LaGuardia and Kennedy Airports. You walk around the model on an elevated catwalk that gradually ascends, so bring binoculars if you have them.

The museum also features a fascinating collection of memorabilia from both the 1964–65 and the 1939–40 World's Fairs and a display of Tiffany lamps manufactured long ago in a nearby Queens factory.

Flushing Meadows-Corona Park, once the location of the extensive ash heaps mentioned in *The Great Gatsby*, is an attraction worth exploring on its own; it has a fine carousel, pleasant small zoo, the recently expanded **Hall of Science**, and the **Unisphere**, centerpiece of the World's Fair. Also, don't miss the city's best Italian ices at the **Lemon Ice King of Corona**, a few steps west of the park (see Secret Ice Cream).

SECRET

MODEL BOATS

On Saturday mornings, the **Model Yacht Club** holds races on the Conservatory Water in Central Park (the boathouse is at Fifth Avenue and 72nd Street, 917-687-7185), an ovoid, brick-lined artificial pond made especially for remote-control toy boats. Some look like sailboats, others like cabin cruisers or tugboats. Watercraft can even be rented at the adjacent boathouse for $10 per hour, but it's almost as much fun just to watch.

SECRET

MUSEUM BARGAINS

For institutions bent on educating the public, New York museums charge an awful lot of money. Regular adult admission is in the $8-to-$10 range, and if you have a whole family to pay for, or want to see several institutions in a day, you'll end up dispensing a fortune. Here are a few ways to ease the financial load.

Thursday and Friday evenings from 5:30 till 8:30 at the **Museum of Modern Art** (11 West 53rd Street, 708-9400), admission is on a "pay what you wish" basis, and what you wish can be as little as 25¢ or a dollar. The crowds can be huge, but dwindle after 7:30. Similarly, the **Whitney Museum of American Art** (945 Madison Avenue, 570-3676) is free on Thursdays from 6 P.M. until 8 P.M. Friday evening is pay-what-you-wish night at the **Guggenheim** (1071 Fifth Avenue, 423-3500), my favorite among the big-deal museums, and not just because of Frank Lloyd Wright's spiraling design (no skateboards allowed).

Many of the museums that occupy public lands are pay-what-you-wish at all times, although they don't encourage you to take advantage of this opportunity, and post their inflated admission prices as if that is what they expect everyone to pay. If you need a justification to give the **Metropolitan Museum of Art** (82nd Street and Fifth Avenue, 535-7710) $2, say, instead of $8, consider the following: The Met continues to annex huge portions of Central Park for its tax-free domain, enjoys public subsidies of other sorts, gets most of its art free from rich people, pays a pittance to those of its employees who actually put in a full workday, and demeans the art on the walls by selling kitschy crap in museum stores that occupy front-and-center locations in its galleries. Besides, the overwhelming crowds certainly diminish your enjoyment of the art, and your ability to look at very much of it during a single visit.

Other museums with the same policy include the **American Museum of Natural History** (79th Street and Central Park West, 769-5100) and the **Brooklyn Museum** (200 Eastern Parkway, Brooklyn, 718-638-5000), a friendlier institution where I never hesitate to pay the $4 asking price and where the museum shops sell a much more interesting line of crap.

SECRET
OASES
❧

Just when the towering skyscrapers of Midtown seem implacable, you'll stumble on an urban oasis — a sliver of space between buildings intensively landscaped with trees, undulating benches, and earthworks that make it seem like a Robert Smithson project. These microparks were often created as a result of concessions granted to owners by the city during the last two decades. It works like this: Joe Developer owns a lot on which he is permitted by the zoning laws to construct a 30-story building with a limited floor area. After negotiating with the city, he is granted the right to build a 45-story tower with increased floor area in exchange for creating a tiny park that he is responsible for maintaining for the public use. As a result of Joe's building, Midtown suffers from reduced light and increased congestion, but pedestrians enjoy an unexpected oasis. I'll let you judge whether the trade-off is worth it.

One of the best of these pocket-sized parks is on the north side of East 51st Street between Second and Third Avenues. Dubbed **Green Acre Park**, it boasts a waterfall, extensive greenery, and even a kiosk selling sandwiches, soups, and beverages at reasonable prices. Another favorite is the unnamed oasis on **East 50th Street between Sixth and Seventh Avenues** that runs all the way through to 49th Street. This one also has a stunning waterfall and a diminutive branch of the soup-and-sandwich joint **Au Bon Pain**, a good place to grab a muffin or juice.

Other, less spectacular oases include the one on **West 46th Street between Fifth and Sixth Avenues**, and another just **east of Fifth Avenue on 53rd Street**. And there are many more in the midtown

area — perfect places to economize on lunch by buying a sandwich at a deli and eating in a shady bower.

SECRET
OBSCURE MUSEUMS
❊

With the current tourism boom, the big famous museums are packed, not only for their separate-admission special shows, but also their regular collections. In the Metropolitan Museum, for example, you will have to crane your neck at any hour of the week to see Botticelli's *Annunciation* and Gauguin's *Two Tahitian Women*; while the Guggenheim was so crowded for the recent motorcycles show that the wait to get in often topped two hours. The solution? Seek out some of the city's more obscure museums, where you can stroll about unimpeded, gaze at the exhibits for as long as you like, and pay an admission price a fraction of what the well-known establishments charge — and sometimes admission is free.

Every day is two-for-one day on **Audubon Terrace** (Broadway and 155th Street), a green patch across the street from Trinity Cemetery in Washington Heights. Two excellent museums vie for your attention. The **American Numismatic Society** (926-2234) has one of the world's largest collections of coins, from which are assembled topical shows like *The World of Coins*, presenting numismatic history in chronological order since 600 BC. The **Hispanic Society of America** (690-0743) exhibits Spanish and Hispanic objects, including paintings and works of decorative art, in a pleasantly musty setting that owes little to contemporary museum design.

The range of materials from Spain is surprisingly large: Roman artifacts, Moorish tiles, and Gothic and Renaissance paintings, including *Juan de Pareja* by Velazquez and many other stunning oil portraits. Admission to both Audubon Terrace museums is free.

The world's largest collection of Fabergé eggs is not in the Louvre or the Hermitage but in the ***Forbes Magazine* Gallery** (62 Fifth Avenue, 620-2200). This excellent free museum contains the collections of the late Malcolm Forbes, whose penchant for accumulating interesting stuff also ran to miniature colonial and Federal-era American rooms, presidential documents and memorabilia, and an idiosyncratic array of toys, including hundreds of toy boats and thousands of tin soldiers, loved by kids and adults alike.

The nonprofit **Asia Society** maintains a pair of galleries at its handsome headquarters at 70th Street and Park Avenue (288-6400) — one for traveling shows and one for its permanent collection — in addition to an auditorium for performances, a library that is open to the public, and an outdoor garden terrace. Exhibition topics have included the tea ceremony in Japanese art, modern Indian painting, Thai sculpture, and Islamic book illustration.

My favorite neglected big museum is the **Museum of the City of New York** (1220 Fifth Avenue, 534-1672). Situated at the upper reaches of Fifth Avenue's Museum Mile, it offers historical exhibits centered on a single city region (like Coney Island, Harlem, or the Broadway Theater District), as well as exhibits of costumes and landscape paintings and photographs. The City Museum also has a wonderful collection of dollhouses, and occasionally mounts one-person shows of contemporary artists and photographers. Just north of it is **El Museo del Barrio** (1230 Fifth Avenue, 831-7272), which presents the art and culture of Puerto Rico, other Caribbean islands, and New York's barrios, or Hispanic neighborhoods.

Looking like a hilltop temple, the **Jacques Marchais Center of Tibetan Art** (338 Lighthouse Road, 718-987-3500) is unexpectedly located on Staten Island. It comprises two picturesque stone buildings that seem as though they were transported from the Himalayas and that house the world's largest collection of Tibetan art, including musical instruments, costumes, and bronze statuary in a sublime garden setting.

SECRET

OPERA

⚘

The whole world knows about the Metropolitan Opera and its lower-rent sibling the City Opera, both conveniently located at Lincoln Center, but fewer patronize the city's smaller opera companies, where would-bes and has-beens congregate with people who just plain love opera on a personal scale. Located on the Bowery, the **Amato Opera** (319 Bowery, 228-8200) has been presenting slightly flawed renditions of the classics for decades. The operas are fully staged with convincing costumes; only the orchestra is slighted — musical backing is usually a piano or trio. With tickets priced under $20, an Amato Opera performance is an affordable treat. Another small-scale company is the **DiCapo Opera Theatre** (184 East 76th Street, 288-9438). Also check publications for free opera presentations in Central Park during the summer, always done with full orchestra but sans costumes.

SECRET

OUTDOOR DINING

❧

Even more than Paris, New York is a city of outdoor cafés. In certain parts of town, where the sidewalks are wide enough to permit it, nearly every restaurant flings a few tables onto the concrete from late April until deep into the autumn. Look for these sidewalk cafés along Broadway and Amsterdam Avenue on the Upper West Side (there are dozens), along Hudson and Bleecker Streets in Greenwich Village, and on Avenue A across the street from Tompkins Square.

But many New Yorkers, like me, disdain to sit on the sidewalk, where you're prey to panhandlers, blowing effluvia, diesel exhaust, and the envious gaze of passersby who do everything but actually grab a bite of your food. Much more pleasant are those establishments that have secret gardens out back, many of them elaborately landscaped with trees, flowers, and even topiary. One favorite is **Le Jardin** (25 Cleveland Place, 343-9599), which serves moderately priced French bistro fare in a tented rear garden hung with grapevines. Another is **Roettele A.G.** (126 East 7th Street, 674-4140), a Swiss joint in the same price range also serving German and Italian food, where a summer supper can be as simple as a bowl of chilled soup with bread and melted raclette. Serving more creative bistro fare is **Grove** (314 Bleecker Street, 675-9463), whose fenced backyard almost merits the adjective "forested."

More expensive is **Caffe Bondi** (7 West 20th Street, 691-8136), dishing up Sicilian chow with interesting North African notes in a serene, European garden just steps from bustling Fifth Avenue. Everyone has been raving about the revamped **Boathouse Café** (East Park Drive and 72nd Street, 517-2233) in Central Park; while expensive, it's still cheaper than the hideous tourist trap **Tavern on the Green** (Central Park West at 67th Street, 873-3200).

Me, I'd rather avoid the tourists entirely and hit one of the cheapo East Village places that sport tenement gardens out back, often furnished with mismatched furniture and combinations of plastic and real flowers. You feel like Jackie Gleason's gonna hang out a window and yell "Shaddup youse"! My favorites are **Sahara East** (184 First Avenue, 353-9000), an Egyptian joint serving great couscous and grilled meats that provides a row of hookahs for its patrons to use ($5; tobacco only, please). The West Village can counter with **Caffe Picasso** (359 Bleecker Street, 929-6232), a wood-burning-oven establishment with excellent pizza and sandwiches. Also check out **Oznot's Dish** (see Secret Williamsburg) in Brooklyn, and **Aesop's Tables** (1233 Bay Street, 718-720-2005) in Staten Island.

SECRET
PASTRY
❀

Let's start at the upper end, for a change. **Payard Patisserie and Bistro** (1032 Lexington Avenue, 717-5252) has a sumptuous dining room clad in dark woods and wraparound glass cases filled with bizarrely colorful and elaborate pastries, rich original creations of fondant, whipped cream, dark chocolate, bits of candied fruit, and puff pastry — not the place to go for a simple cream puff or Italian cannoli. Also in a French vein, but incorporating many American elements, is **Bouley Bakery** (120 West Broadway, 964-2525), a temporary substitute for the acclaimed restaurant Bouley, which closed last summer and is supposed to reopen in 1999. In addition to great breads, Bouley features loaf-sized meringues studded with nuts, sublime madeleines, perfect cookies, fruit tarts, and, in the dining room, an array of pricey but excellent soups and sandwiches and more elaborate main courses. At both Payard and Bouley, you can easily stroll in and carry out, but reserve well in advance if you want to dine at either.

On a less elevated level, New York boasts many great pastry shops, among them **Marquet** (15 East 12th Street, 229-9313), a slavish re-creation of a French patisserie done by a Brooklyn couple. The croissants, pains au chocolat, brioches, cakes, and fruit-filled pastries are rhapsodically good, and the coffee ain't bad, either. There are many daily luncheon plates, which run to cold meats or cured fish with cornichons and salad; some hot selections are thrown in. Marquet is an absolute gem.

One of the quirkiest places in town is **City Bakery** (22 East 17th Street, 366-1414), a hip joint just off the Union Square Farmers Market decorated with pastry boxes marching up the walls to the stratospheric ceiling. The bakery's claim to fame is its tarts, which have such fillings as rich crème brûlée flecked with vanilla bean, Indian pudding, and, the tartest tart of all, lemon. City Bakery puts on a hot-cocoa festival every winter, variations changing daily. Its homemade marshmallows attract kids from miles around.

Of the Italian pastry shops in town, many dating from the turn of the century, the best is clearly **Veniero's** (342 East 11th Street, 674-4415), located in what used to be the Italian East Village. The miniature pastries, available by the pound, are a particular delight and a bargain to boot. The roster includes chocolate and vanilla cannolis, sfogliatelle, cream puffs, berry tarts, and éclairs. Large versions are also available, but you'll be hard pressed to choose. Of the cakes, my favorite is zuppa inglese, a white wedding cake filled with rum-laced chocolate and whipped cream.

Outside Manhattan, there are too many good pastry shops to mention — each ethnic enclave in Queens, for example, has one or two, ranging from the German konditerei of Ridgewood and Middle Village, to the Chinese cake shops of Flushing, to the glitzy Greek bakeries of Astoria. My favorite in the Bronx is **Madonia Brothers** (2348 Arthur Avenue, 718-295-5573), just down the street from the Arthur Avenue Market (see Secret Markets), where the specialty is cannolis filled right when you order them with the lightest ricotta cream imaginable, studded with little bits of candied fruit. Thus, the shell stays crisp — which is not the case when the cannolis are prefilled and sit for days in the refrigerator case. Finding a place that fills its cannoli shells to order isn't easy; one that does in Manhattan is **Rocco's Pastry** (243 Bleecker Street, 242-6031).

S E C R E T

PERFORMANCE ART

⚜

Occupying shaky territory somewhere between theater and conceptual art is performance art. It's been a favorite night out for downtown hipsters for the last 15 years. The premier space for this sort of activity is PS 122 (150 First Avenue, 477-5288, Web site: www. ps122.org), founded in 1979 in a former public school; now the PS stands for "performance space." There are currently two theaters in the building. Downstairs, I recently saw Elevator Repair Service, a comic troupe that mixes the disciplines of synchronized dance with stand-up and sketch comedy; a great deal of yoga is thrown in too as performers wedge themselves into a small wooden box. Upstairs, renowned (in New York, at least) porn actress Annie Sprinkle performed. She provided running commentary while screening clips of films that spanned her professional career. These days, PS 122 often goes mainstream, featuring performers like monologists Spalding Gray and Eric Bogosian.

Even more small-scale and avant garde than PS 122 is **Dixon Place** (258 Bowery, 219-3088, Web site: www.dixonplace.org), dedicated to supporting and encouraging new performance artists in its cluttered space on the Bowery, which seems like a friend's comfy living room (with battered furniture to match). Admission prices are kept well below $10. Dance-inflected performances are often delivered by members of the resident dance company, the School of Hard Knocks; comedy- and drama-oriented performers from all over the country are attracted to the space as well. I recently saw the performance company from Seattle called Five Lesbian Brothers, which regaled an appreciative audience with a multipart, gender-bending fable bearing a feminist message.

SECRET

PERIODICALS

❖

New York is such a complex and mercurial metropolis that even the most hip can claim to know only a fraction of what's going on. But what all of them have in common is knowing what tools will keep them abreast. These tools are periodicals. One won't do; you'll have to scan all that are mentioned here to make an informed decision about how to blow any particular evening.

I'm partial to the *Village Voice*, of course. That's the paper I write for. Founded in the '50s by Norman Mailer, Dan Wolf, and pals, the publication is closely associated with Greenwich Village and has particularly good coverage of movies — in fact, it reviews everything that comes out, from big-budget productions to the tiniest auteur releases. The pullout *Choices* minimagazine is a densely packed guide to film, dance, rock and jazz, art, photography, and general, unclassifiable "happenings" in the Open City section. The *Voice* is published every Wednesday. Grab a free copy from the red plastic street-corner boxes or from the pile in front of many newsstands.

Also free (look for it in the green boxes every Tuesday evening) is the *New York Press* While the political perspective of the *Voice* is leftist and beatnik, the *Press*'s is generally right of center, a product of '70s neoconservatism. But there's plenty to love about the quirky, confessional style of some *Press* writers, even though they tend to drone on. The *Press* also features a concise listings section, although it doesn't pull out, so you'll have to lug the whole paper around with you.

A third source of downtown, art-scene-oriented coverage is *Time Out New York*, which likes to be called by its acronym, TONY. It's an offshoot of a quintessential London publication, and features the most intensive listings-style information of any of the periodicals; virtually no other editorial content gets in the way. Unfortunately, it costs $2.50, partly because it's presented in a glossy magazine format rather than as a tabloid. Get it at newsstands and in specialty shops.

More upscale events with a decidedly Uptown perspective will be found in *New York* magazine, which comes out weekly on Monday and will cost you a whopping $2.95. It's tops for celebrity gossip and museum-oriented coverage, and throws in a few muck-raking local stories (favorite topics: shrinks, City Hall scandals, stockbrokers, private schools). A few years back, *New York* swallowed *Cue* magazine, which still functions as a magazine-within-a-magazine and furnishes the event listings. *New York* is especially good if you're looking for restaurant openings — these are generally listed here first. Less dependable if you're searching for something to do on a particular evening is the *New Yorker* (Monday publication), which costs about the same amount. You may prefer it, though, since after you've used its listings you may want to keep it for its literary content and its read-yourself-to-sleep value.

Don't neglect the dailies, either. The Friday *New York Times* and *Daily News* both have extensive detachable weekend sections that list events and provide movie and restaurants reviews. These papers are great if you're only interested in the coming weekend. The Wednesday *Times* is the place to look for restaurant reviews and coverage of New York's burgeoning foodie scene.

Since New York is a recycling city, you'll often find piles of newspapers and magazines in front of apartment buildings, and these can be scavenged for almost-new copies of many of the above publications; it's an easy way to keep up without spending a bundle.

SECRET
PHOTOGRAPHY

✤

Arguably the photography capital of the United States, New York boasts myriad galleries devoted exclusively to shutterbugging, and at any given time there are two dozen or more photo shows to be seen around town. The **International Center of Photography**, or

ICP (Fifth Avenue and 94th Street, 860-1777), founded by Cornell Capa and occupying a striking townhouse opposite Central Park, has three exhibitions going at once. Recently, the shows included Walker Evans's lesser-known New York 35-millimeter snapshots and large-format New England photos, views of Coney Island by Harvey Stein, and a project called *Intimate City* by Thomas Roma — a series on African American urban life. A Midtown branch of the center, where three additional shows are usually presented, is located at 1133 Avenue of the Americas and shares the same info phone. You may visit both for a single admission charge.

The publisher **Aperture** (20 East 23rd Street, 505-5555), founded in 1952 by Minor White and famous for its once-daring monographs of Alvarez Bravo, Sally Mann, and Diane Arbus, maintains a bookstore that peddles its publications, including back issues of its quarterly, and the **Burden Gallery** (20 East 23rd Street, 505-5555), which presents shows based on recent books, like Linda Troeller's *Healing Waters*, luminous color interiors of European spas.

Other influential spaces include the photo gallery at the **Museum of Modern Art** (11 West 53rd Street, 708-9400), but look to the private commercial galleries like **PaceWildensteinMacGill** (32 East 57th Street, 759-7999) and the **Witkin Gallery** (415 West Broadway, 925-5510) for some of the most exciting contemporary shows and free admission. Consult the *Village Voice*'s pullout *Choices* for the most extensive photography coverage.

Collectors of photo books new and used will want to visit **A Photographer's Place** (133 Mercer Street, 431-9358). The best place to buy a camera at a discount is **B & H Photo** (420 Ninth Avenue, 444-6608, Web site: www.bhphotovideo.com); to have one repaired, try **Swiss Camera** (38 West 32nd Street, 594-6340).

SECRET

PICKLES

❧

You'll never crave pickles from a jar again once you've tasted **Guss' Pickles** (35 Essex Street, 254-4477), the last remaining pickle vendor on this stretch of Essex. The brine-soaked beauties are splayed across the Lower East Side sidewalk in 55-gallon barrels, marshaled according to how long they've been soaking: new (a day or two), half-sour (two or three days), and sour (over three days). The sour, especially, produce a prodigious pucker, but my favorites are the new pickles, which retain the crunch of the kirby cuke while tasting powerfully of garlic and coriander seed. There's no vinegar or dill in sight. A quart costs $4.25, and, packed in brine, they gradually become more sour. Also buy pickled tomatoes, mixed vegetables, sauerkraut, and several types of olives. Ask for a free taste of any product.

SECRET

PICKUP SCENES

❧

Whether you're looking for a boy or a girl, consult the following list of tried-and-true places to pick one up — that is, if you prefer to boycott the bar and coffeehouse scene.

Barnes & Noble superstores, with their loungy and brainy atmosphere and two-person reading tables, are a magnet for those on the prowl and their rightful prey. In late mornings and early evenings on the weekends, the branch at Union Square (33 East 17th Street, 253-0810) comes alive with singles who judge each other by what they're reading. For my money, Travel and Cookbooks are the two best sections.

Central Park is always a wholesome place to meet people, especially in the Sheep Meadow or Belvedere Castle, though you might want to avoid the Ramble, where you're likely to see couples, both homo and hetero, already getting it on.

At weekday movie matinees, the crowds are sparse and composed mainly of singles in a mellow mood with the rest of the day to kill. Romantic pictures are your best bet, of course, if you're lookin' for a gal. Boys encountered at science-fiction films may not be at the highest level of emotional maturity. No one over 18 years old will be found at a Leonardo di Caprio film. That said, the best cinemas for pickup are the **Film Forum** and the **Angelika** (see Secret Cinemas).

A few other opportunities: Have lunch at any crowded Chinese restaurant on Mott Street and you'll be seated at a table with lots of other people. Offer to share a ride with someone you see hailing a cab who seems to be going in the same direction. Street fairs, which occur during the spring, summer, and fall with depressing regularity, are a magnet for singles with no agenda. Scout the coffeehouses and tea parlors in the area beforehand, and you'll be able to use "Would you like to get a cup of coffee?" as your pickup line.

SECRET
PIERCINGS
⚜

Piercing, like other forms of creative mutilation — such as branding, tattooing, and, the latest fad, fantasy plastic surgery — has been undergoing a tremendous surge of popularity in New York during the last decade. Piercing parlors now line St. Marks Place, lewdly offering to pierce clitoris, testicles, and nipples in addition to the more common ears, nose, and (painful and very slow to heal) belly button. The method involves an air gun that fires sealed and sterile bolts into flesh; it's nearly painless and supposedly prevents transmission of HIV and the dreaded, newly discovered hepatitis C. But these piercing stalls are operated by shopkeepers of uncertain hygiene, and who wants to be pierced in the public thoroughfare, shielded from the gaze of curious idlers by a flimsy gauze curtain?

Accordingly, I'd advise visiting the piercing professionals at **Gauntlet** (144 Fifth Avenue, 229-0180), which has been in business since 1975 and where friends of mine have had nearly every bit of skin, private as well as public, pierced. To preview their services and charges, check out their Web site (www.gauntlet.com). Other reliable parlors are **New York Adorned** (47 Second Avenue, 473-0007), which also tattoos and henna tattoos; and **Venus Modern Body Arts** (199 East 4th Street, 473-1954), which describes its service as "precision body piercing." They won't miss your belly button, if that's where they're aiming.

But, as my 11-year-old daughter discovered when she showed up at her pediatrician's office for her annual checkup with three earrings in one ear and was admonished for having had it done in a shop, any physician is probably willing to do piercings for about the same fee as a piercing parlor. The disadvantage is that you have to bring your own jewelry; the advantage is that a doctor can dispense anesthetics unavailable to nondoctors and can prescribe follow-up antibiotics, as necessary.

SECRET

RICE

✦

Kalustyan's (123 Lexington Avenue, 685-3451), a Lebanese/Armenian grocery with one of the best collections of Indian, Middle Eastern, and Persian products in the city, has a mind-blowing display of rice. On a recent visit I counted 20 varieties, offered in small, one-pound packages so you can buy a selection. From fat-grained Turkish rice, to odiferous basmati, to Thai sticky, to sinister black rice, you'll see varieties you never knew existed. This shop in the midst of Curry Hill (see Secret Indian) also has bargain prices on nuts, spices, and dried fruits; a carryout section in the back with some of the best tabouli in town; and a great selection of cookbooks right behind the register.

The restaurant called **Rice** (227 Mott Street, 226-5775) offers just that in many Asian and Middle Eastern variations. Pick a plain rice like Japanese short grain or Tibetan red with a one-dollar topping such as mango or avocado salsa, or select more elaborate rice-based dishes like Thai grilled beef over rice or Indian curry chicken over rice. The menu is rounded out with rice puddings and pastries.

SECRET

ROCK CLUBS

✦

New York is simply the best American city in which to see live rock music. The top acts play multiple dates at the bigger venues; up-and-coming bands from out of town would kill for a date here;

English and Canadian bands find it the cheapest and most prestigious American city to get to. The differing aspirations and salary requirements of bands have created a system of tiered venues involving dozens of clubs — it would take a whole book to detail the economics and sociology involved. Here is a thumbnail sketch of the club system.

On the lowest level of the food chain are the clubs that book local talent and barely known traveling acts from around the country aiming to make it big. Of course, a handful of these bands will actually hit the jackpot, and these joints provide you with a chance to see them as they will never be seen again — at the height of their raw power in an intimate setting. The most fabled of these clubs, CBGB/OMFUG (315 Bowery, 420-8392), the original punk venue, was built by country-and-western maven Hilly Kristal. It was also gigging ground zero for late-'70s stars Blondie, Talking Heads, Dead Boys, and the Ramones. Anyone interested in the history of rock will want to make a pilgrimage into its filthy, beer-stinking interior, lovingly preserved in its original splendor, although booking policies now favor sardining in as many low-paid, undertalented bands per evening as possible and counting on friends of band members to fill up the club. The music and ambiance is generally much better at CBGB's Gallery (313 Bowery, 677-0455) right next door.

A couple of fave outlets for local talent are the **Mercury Lounge** (217 East Houston Street, 260-4700), which has a killer sound system, and its new sibling, the **Bowery Ballroom** (6 Delancey Street, 533-2111). More intimate and neighborhoody is **Brownies** (169 Avenue A, 420-8392), while **Coney Island High** (15 St. Marks Place, 674-7959) is a larger, bilevel space appealing to a punky bridge-and-tunnel crowd. Experimental rock is vented at the **Knitting Factory** (74 Leonard Street, 219-3006). Put on your headband

and tie-dyes to visit **Wetlands** (161 Hudson Street, 966-4225), the retro-hippie venue in Tribeca where the Spin Doctors got their start. The joint has landed on my permanent shit list — I was kicked out a few years ago for smoking a joint (something you can traditionally get by with at most rock clubs) — but it does provide a convenient segue into the next category of clubs, the ones that host big traveling acts in addition to local bands.

These venues are not much larger than those on the previous tier, but they have a more formal, even stuffy, air. They are the showcase clubs where hopeful, much-buzzed bands vie with slumming big or once-big acts to kiss the asses of record company execs who sit in roped-off areas and feast off their abundant expense accounts. The **Bottom Line** (15 West 4th Street, 228-6300) is the most famous, located in the midst of the New York University campus. A recent week of attractions included Al Stewart, Robyn Hitchcock, and Buster Poindexter (the nom de guerre of ex-New York Dolls member David Johanssen). The space is mainly sit-down, and two shows per evening are scheduled. If you line up just before a set you may get standing room near the bar, thus avoiding the two-drink minimum. In Chelsea, **Tramps** (51 West 21st Street, 544-1666) furnishes an intimate setting for the likes of David Crosby, Merle Haggard, King Sunny Adé, and the Meters; tickets are priced at about $20.

The next club tier contains the ballrooms — ancient, elegant dance halls that once hosted the big bands. The premier uptown venue is **Roseland** (239 West 52nd Street); downtown it's **Irving Plaza** (17 Irving Place). The concert information line for both is 777-1224. Impecunious idiots (sometimes including me) who like to blow extra money buy their tickets from **Ticketmaster** (307-7171), which slaps on all sorts of extra charges. Wise guys with time on their hands go right to the Irving Plaza box office (Monday through Saturday,

12 P.M. to 6 P.M.), where no charges are added. Recent acts that have graced these ballrooms include Ziggy Marley, Iron Maiden (yes, heavy metal still exists), and God Street Wine. In the same size range is the wonderful **Hammerstein Ballroom** (311 West 34th Street, 279-7740), newly constructed to resemble a nineteenth-century opera house, where I recently saw Prodigy. Once again, Ticketmaster hawks the tickets, but there's also a box office on the premises where supplemental charges can be avoided. Rock shows, mainly of the soft variety, are occasionally hosted at **Radio City Music Hall** (1260 Avenue of the Americas, 247-4777); here you can also fulfill the touristic objective of viewing this amazing Art Deco pile from the inside.

Then there are the arenas, like Manhattan's **Madison Square Garden** and New Jersey's **Continental Arena**. But by the time an act hits this tier I'd rather just buy the CD. How to navigate the confusing array of clubs and find those places too new to be mentioned in this totally up-to-date book? The *Voice*, the *New York Press*, and *Time Out* all offer reliable critics' choices for the upcoming week.

SECRET
ROLLER COASTER
❖

The **Cyclone** may be the last great roller coaster left in Gotham, but it's a doozy. Located in Coney Island's Astroland, this coaster is 3,200 feet long, hits a maximum speed of 68 miles per hour, and boasts nine drops of which the largest is a hair-raising 90 feet. Although many bigger and more impressive theme coasters have been built in suburban amusement parks — turning passengers upside down and every which way — there's nothing like a rickety wood coaster to give one the heebie-jeebies, a feeling accentuated by the shaky and bumpy ride.

The Cyclone first flew on 26 June 1927 after being assembled from parts manufactured in Brooklyn, Manhattan, and Queens. Charles Lindbergh was an early and enthusiastic customer, claiming the ride was scarier than his famed transatlantic flight. Although the original price of a ride was 25¢, it now costs $4 — it operates daily in summer and weekends only in late spring and early fall. If you want more information, or would like to look at dramatic pictures of the Cyclone in action, check out the following Web sites: coneyisland. brooklyn.ny.us/framesite/indexwindow.html *and* www.astroland.com.

A couple of blocks north on the Riegelmann Boardwalk (see Secret Boardwalks) you'll see the rusting hulk of another nearly identical coaster, the **Thunderbolt**, completed two years earlier than the Cyclone for the Steeplechase amusement park. The Thunderbolt lacked the safety features that were incorporated into the Cyclone; in its first season of operation there were many accidents, including one fatality. Under the Thunderbolt you'll see a rotting frame structure that was once a hotel. The edifice was featured prominently in the Woody Allen film *Radio Days*.

SECRET

RUSSIAN

❖

Known as Little Odessa, Brooklyn's **Brighton Beach** is thronged with immigrants from Russia, Georgia, and the Ukraine. The board-walk comes alive here on summer evenings. Russian performers sing and play tear-jerking standards on the accordion while neighbor-hood residents promenade in their Sunday best. The boardwalk cafés sling their tables onto the wooden thoroughfare and offer cheap, homestyle eats like kharcho, a soup of rice and lamb laced with dill, and chicken tabaka, a nearly boneless bird fried with lots of garlic till the skin is supremely crisp. Fresh seafood also excels, especially flounder and sturgeon shish kebab. My favorite among these joints is **Caffe Volna** (3145 Brighton Street, 718-332-0341), but the food is nearly the same at all of them.

The main drag of Little Odessa is Brighton Beach Avenue, a block or two inland from the boardwalk, depending on where you leave it. Under the shadow of the elevated tracks, this artery is mobbed with shoppers who sweep in and out of Russian delis, coffee shops, clothiers, off-price vegetable stands, and establishments that pack and ship the stuff back home. There are also 20 or so big-ticket combination nightclub/restaurants like the National and the Odessa, which can provide an expensive and disorienting experience for the non-Russian. One of the most user-friendly featuring the requisite floorshow is **Primorski** (282 Brighton Beach Avenue, 718-891-3111), where Russian food with a Georgian bent is served, including hearty soups, dumplings, blini with caviar (skip it), chicken Kiev, and fresh fish.

On a more plebian culinary level, keep your eye peeled for the carts that sell pieroshki — deep-fried turnovers stuffed with potato, cabbage, or cheese, usually priced at 50¢ each. Summer and winter there's one in front of **Taste of Russia** (219 Brighton Beach Avenue) next to a table laden with cakes and other pastries. Pop into the neighborhood's only Russian supermarket, **M & I International Foods** (249 Brighton Beach Avenue, 718-615-1011). At the head of the street, where the elevated turns for its final run to Coney Island, is **Mrs. Stahl Knishes** (1001 Brighton Beach Avenue, 718-648-0210), open since 1935 and one of the few vestiges of the Jewish community that dominated this quarter for most of the century. The store sells about a dozen types of knish (a fist-sized, thin-crusted, cubic pie with fillings like potato, pineapple-cheese, sweet potato, and kasha, a coarse grain with a dark and smoky flavor, not to be missed) for $1.50 each.

Manhattan has its share of expensive Russian restaurants, of which the most notorious is currently **Firebird** (365 West 46th Street, 586-0244), situated in an elegantly appointed townhouse, with costumed doormen and walls decorated with memorabilia. The prix-fixe pretheater dinner is the best value.

SECRET
SAMPLE SALES

❧

Salespeople for clothing manufacturers generally pay for their own samples. When the season is done, these samples are sold — sometimes by the salesmen and saleswomen themselves. November-December and May-June are the most common times for these sales, following the spring-summer and fall-winter seasons, respectively, though they can also occur at other times. The best way to track down sales is to hang out in the Garment District, extending from 34th to 40th Streets, between Sixth and Ninth Avenues. Hawkers pass out handbills directing you to musty lofts where the goods are peddled. Sometimes the more prestigious manufacturers host sales in their corporate offices. Either way, attending such sales is a good way to get an inside view of the garment industry. Prices will typically be about one-quarter to one-half of retail. The drawback is that you can't try the merchandise on, nor can you return it if you're dissatisfied. And cash is usually the only means of payment accepted.

A company called sss/**Nice Price** (134 West 37th Street, 947-8748, Web site: www.clothingline.com) has revolutionized the sample-sale business by providing a permanent space that hosts sales on a rotating basis. A recorded phone message lists its current sales, or you can preview upcoming sales at its Web site. Major credit cards are accepted.

S E C R E T
SANCTUARY

❖

The **General Theological Seminary of the Episcopal Church** (175 Ninth Avenue, 243-5150) occupies some of Chelsea's most appealing acreage — an entire city block between 21st and 22nd Streets consisting of several buildings circled like a wagon train around a series of well-landscaped spaces. This relaxing sanctuary is open to the public from noon till 3 P.M. Monday through Saturday. It's a great place for reading or quiet relaxation, but you must sign in at the entrance.

St. Luke's in the Fields (487 Hudson Street, 924-0562), located in Greenwich Village, isn't in the fields anymore, but the neighborhood still has a nineteenth-century feel to it, and the church grounds contain a delightful garden, which most people view through an

ornate wrought-iron fence. The garden is open to the public, however. Enter at the front of the church, which dates back to 1822,
making it one of the oldest chapels in New York. Go behind the
chapel and veer to the left to approach the garden, which is filled
with flowers in summer and dotted with comfortable wooden
benches.

S E C R E T

SECONDHAND CLOTHES

✧

A boho friend of mine — whose day job involves filing and
photocopying — wouldn't think of setting foot outside his East 13th
Street digs unless he was dressed head to toe in '40s attire: pleated
gabardine pants, wing tips, flimsy-collared shirts, and skinny ties.
His wardrobe occupies several rooms of his spacious, rent-controlled
apartment, which he's spent 10 years decorating; it's now a dream
palace that he would never leave if he didn't have to go to work —
or shop.

He buys his clothes at **Domsey's** (431 Kent Avenue, Brooklyn,
718-384-6000), the Williamsburg warehouse stuffed with so many
retro clothes that its employees periodically bale up the excess and
ship it to Africa. In the back of the store, you can buy used clothes
by the pound. And, of course, '40s is not the only style available —
you can do any decade you like. Another Williamsburg mainstay is

D & G Thriftshop (873 Broadway, Brooklyn, 718-452-5686), where furniture is also hawked and the clothes are piled in amorphous heaps instead of racked.

With firsthand clothing prices soaring and the Gap upscaling so that a cotton shirt often costs $50 or more, your only choices for inexpensive duds may be **Old Navy**, **Conway** (all over Midtown, call 967-5300 for locations), or the thrifts. Increasingly, hipsters are accessorizing or dressing entirely in secondhand clothes, even more so since the popular resurgence of swing-type musical ensembles. Other places to score these threads include the multiple **Salvation Army** locations, the best of which are at 208 Eighth Avenue (929-5214) in Manhattan's Chelsea, 26 East 125th Street (289-9617) in Harlem, and, mother of them all, 34–02 Steinway Street (718-472-2414) in the eastern part of Astoria, Queens.

Of course, for the lazy there's also a plethora of "antique clothing" stores whose owners, by also shopping at Domsey's, do the winnowing for you; these establishments present their wares in attractive displays and charge four or five times the Domsey's price. These joints are also more likely to favor kitsch clothing, like bowling shirts (sometimes fake) with the name "Ralph" embroidered over the pocket, or bomber jackets in suspiciously perfect condition. Nevertheless, when my high-school-age nephews and nieces fly in from Wisconsin, it's to these comfortable places they'd rather go. Most popular is the **Antique Boutique** (712 Broadway, 460-8830), but my favorite is **Tokyo Joe** (334 East 11th Street, 473-0724, and 240 East 28th Street, 532-2605), frequented by Japanese hipsters, who often affect retro-clothing looks.

SECRET
SEX
⚜

Only a year ago, destinations like Times Square in Manhattan and Queens Boulevard in Queens were rife with topless clubs, peep shows, and lewd video parlors. Then the puritanical Mayor Giuliani invented a way to get rid of them. While freedom-of-speech guarantees precluded outlawing pornography per se, he discovered in the course of a three-year court battle that he could wield city zoning restrictions to chase purveyors away from their traditional areas by specifying that they must be no less than 500 feet from the nearest domicile, school, or religious institution. Accordingly, most of the Times Square establishments either closed down or adhered to the new order that their stock must be less than 40% pornographic. These establishments were expected to reopen in dark and dreary industrial areas such as West 14th Street's meat market or Brooklyn's Williamsburg and Red Hook, but so far that hasn't happened. Cynics believe that Giuliani undertook his campaign not for the moral edification of the community (it is rumored that Giuliani himself has a mistress), but to free up more real estate for the continued Disneyfication of Times Square.

But sex is a river that can be damned but never dammed. The back pages of the *New York Press* and the *Village Voice* (see Secret Periodicals) are filled with ads for "massage services," out-call prostitutes, and plain old cathouses, many apparently under the protection of the police department, as demonstrated by a recent scandal at the Midtown South Precinct, where nearly 20 officers are under investigation for hanging out, sleeping, and just plain screwing at a nearby whorehouse in exchange for protection. *Screw* magazine, a weekly tabloid published in New York, has been offering lurid advice and running sex advertisements for 25 years, and it's not about to stop now. Pornographic magazines of every stripe are visible on city newsstands, and bookstores like **Virgin** (1540 Broadway, 921-1020) in Times Square and **St. Marks Bookshop** (31 Third Avenue, 260-7853) in the East Village sell coffee-table volumes printed in Germany and Japan that would bring a blush to the most worldly cheek, while **Tower Books** (383 Lafayette Street, 228-5100), also in the East Village, purveys limited-circulation sex fanzines, tattoo mags, as well as no-holds-barred (or maybe I should say "all-holes-bared") piercing publications. **Kim's Video** (6 St. Marks Place, 505-0311) rents the bluest videos; the store is also known for its wide-ranging selection of art films. Here no one will give you a second look when you rent the classic *Teenage Piss Party*.

The swinger clubs of 15 years ago, like Plato's Retreat, have long since closed down, victims of the AIDS scare. Well, almost. There's still one left: **Le Trapeze** (17 East 27th Street, 532-0298), where the swingers are mainly in their forties, and you can't get in without a (heterosexual) date. Or create your own swinger scene by consulting the Multiples section of the personal ads in the *Village Voice*. **Michele Capozzi** (580-2219) offers sex tours of the city by car — promising you won't be disappointed — at a price to be negotiated based on exoticism and duration, as recently reported by *Time Out*, which also has its share of sex ads.

Finally, if you want an old-fashioned topless bar, check out **Billy's Topless** (729 Sixth Avenue, no phone), where the Giuliani restrictions have caused the dancers to cover up but where the old grit still remains. If you want to amuse or offend your friends, shop at **Masterbakers** (511 East 12th Street, 475-0476), where you can order a cake in the shape of a penis or vagina. See also Secret Burlesque and Secret Erotic Toys.

S E C R E T
SKATING
❧

Few things in Manhattan are as exhilarating as sweeping across the ice at the **Wollman Rink** (Central Park East at 62nd Street, 396-1010) with the Midtown skyscrapers towering above. And it's a bargain, too — less than $10 for unlimited time and skate rental. The season begins earlier than you'd imagine, usually on 15 October, and extends through the end of March, weather permitting. Evenings are especially thrilling, when the city lights twinkle like a million stars.

Rockefeller Center's famous ice (Fifth Avenue at 49th Street, 332-7654) can also be accessed for a low price, although the rink is smaller and consequently more crowded. For those who prefer space to twirl or just skate fast, the little-known **Lasker Rink** (Lenox Avenue at 110th Street, 396-1010) charges patrons only about $7, including skate rental, and boasts a hilly setting on the northwest corner of Central Park. One of the most stunning skating facilities in the city is the **World's Fair Skating Rink** (Flushing Meadows-Corona Park, 718-271-1996), which also sponsors a skating school (718-592-6200).

The only ice open year-round is **Sky Rink** at Chelsea Piers (Hudson River at 23rd Street, 336-6100); certain times are reserved for hockey players.

SECRET

SOUP

❖

Food fads break out like brushfires, sweeping in overnight and dominating entire regions of the city. Ten years ago, popcorn created a sensation, and popcorn stores opened all over Midtown selling the stuff in dozens of flavors — like coconut, bubble gum, and tutti frutti — then shut down almost immediately. Other fads have included buffalo chicken wings; pretzels with gooey stuffings; burritos and their bastard offspring, wraps; and sushi, which has stayed with us longer than any other.

Spawned by the *Seinfeld* "Soup Nazi" episode, and in emulation of **Soup Kitchen International** (259A West 55th Street, 757-7330), at least 20 soup-only storefronts have sprung up, of which **Daily Soup** has the most locations. The formula is simple: each offers ten or so pottages per day in carryout containers in a variety of sizes. The price always seems a little steep, but the soup comes with a hunk of bread, piece of fruit, and tiny square of decent chocolate, making it seem like a full meal.

The best is way Downtown: **Souperman** (77 Pearl Street, 269-5777), founded by a celebrity chef who quarreled with his backers and decided to chuck it all and just make soup. My favorite is spicy Mexican ($4.50, $5.95, $10), crammed with kernels of corn right off the cob, chicken, and mild chiles in a tomato base, finished at the last moment with a dollop of sour cream and a few pieces of ripe avocado.

SECRET
STRANGE STORES
❧

One of the virtues of a very large city is that it fosters specialty stores that sell a narrow range of quirky merchandise. Only a city of millions could support so many strange establishments. Here are a few favorites.

Ahoy mate! **New York Nautical Instrument** (140 West Broadway, 962-4522), in addition to carrying antique and modern charts and maps, specializes in old instruments that easily double as objets d'art. If you crave a battered brass diving helmet, it's yours. Or, if you harbor a fantasy that you're the pilot standing on the bridge of the *Titanic*, you can buy an ancient ship's throttle inscribed "Quarter," "Half," and "Full Speed Ahead."

The **Detective Store International** (173 Christopher Street, 366-6466, Web site: www.citysearch.com/nyc/spystore) concentrates on wiretapping and surveillance equipment, binoculars, and other paraphernalia of the trade. Shop here if you'd like to do your own detective work, or merely want to snoop on your neighbors. Unfortunately, during a bust last year lots of illegal equipment was confiscated, and this shop is now a shadow of its former self. Another store, astonishingly, covers the same territory. The **Spy Shop at Quark** (537 Third Avenue, 889-1808) offers night-vision binoculars, video cameras hidden inside light fixtures, booby-trapped briefcases, telephone scramblers, a bug detector in a pen, and rather grand-sounding "kidnap recovery systems."

On a lighter note, **Just Bulbs** (938 Broadway, 228-7820) functions as a lightbulb museum, with many rare and unusual varieties for sale. Can't find the right bulb for that lamp you bought in Beijing?

Here's the place. **Alphaville** (226 West Houston Street, 675-6185) specializes in toys from the '50s and '60s, like Captain Astro metal lunch boxes ($250), original Cooties from the '40s through the '60s ($11.95 per Cootie), and Lone Ranger comics ($28). Actually, quite a few stores confine themselves to antique toys, including **Classic Toys** (218 Sullivan Street, 674-4434), where you'll find model cars and toy soldiers, and **Love Saves the Day** (119 Second Avenue, 228-3802), with kitschy fashion dolls, peacenik curiosities, and gag gifts. Find similar stuff at **Little Ricky** (49 First Avenue, 505-6467), one of the best places in town to buy cheap gifts that scream "I bought this in New York!"

For honky-tonk angels, **Whiskey Dust** (526 Hudson Street, 691-5576) stocks a vast collection of used cowboy boots (!), with snakeskin styles running as high as $300. They've also got western shirts, belts, pants, chaps — all for rent as well as for sale. Go whole hog and rent a replica six-shooter and a bandoleer to go with it. Just don't go into a bank with them, or you may find yourself riddled with real lead.

The customers of **Red Caboose** (23 West 45th Street, 575-0155), which sells new and used Lionel and American Flyer trains, are more likely to be adults than children. Brooklyn's **Train World** (751 McDonald Avenue, 718-436-7072) sells similar merchandise, but its location under an elevated train in a dusty, little-visited part of town makes it infinitely more romantic.

Finally, if you are a fan of the late artist Keith Haring, his work lives on at **Pop Shop** (292 Lafayette Street, 219-2784, Web site: www. haring.com), where you can get the famous crawling baby, barking dog, and three-eyed laughing guy logos emblazoned on everything from T-shirts to pencil cases.

SECRET
SUBWAY
☙

For the cost of a token ($1.50), or one swipe of the Metrocard, you can take unlimited rides on the New York City subway system — assuming you never leave the confines of that system. In fact, aiming to get into the *Guinness Book of World Records*, daredevils regularly compete to see who can ride the entire 722 miles in the shortest amount of time (the current record is something over 24 hours). Here is a quirky guide to the delights of the city's far-flung subway system.

Safety issues first. The subway has received a bad rap in the press and many tourists are afraid to ride. The truth is that the underground railway is one of the city's safer forms of transportation — much safer than taking a cab — especially if you take some precautions. After you descend and pay your fare, if you find that the platform is empty wait near the token booth for a train to arrive (all stations have attended booths). When boarding, choose a car that has plenty of people in it. Avoid riding alone on the more obscure routes to and from the boroughs after midnight and before 6 A.M. You're safe if you take a companion or two with you. Also, don't display expensive jewelry or take your wallet out and fiddle with money or credit cards. These are common-sense precautions that apply in any large city in the world.

Subways sometimes travel for stretches above ground and in the process provide spectacular views of the city. The **B and D trains** get to Brooklyn by going over the Manhattan Bridge on the East River, allowing passengers to look right in through the windows of Chinatown sweatshops and then to compare the skylines of

Downtown and Midtown while enjoying the river from a bird's perspective. The D then runs in a trench the length of Brooklyn before surfacing at Brighton Beach and running along the ocean-front to arrive at Coney Island. Oh! the smell of the salt air when the doors slide open.

The **F train**, which also ends up at Coney Island, makes an unexpected swoop above ground between the Carroll Street and Seventh Avenue stations in Brooklyn, making for amazing views of New York's Upper Bay on the south and the vast expanse of Brooklyn on the north. Best sight: The "KenTilE" sign soaring above the morass of the Gowanus Canal.

The **4 train** is elevated in parts of the Bronx, as are the **2 and 5 trains**, permitting glimpses of working-class life in the tenements that flank the tracks, often from as little as 20 feet away. The 2 and 5 furnish evidence that the South Bronx, which was almost totally burned out as recently as 10 years ago, is now resurging — witness the renovated apartment buildings and, just north of the Freeman Avenue stop, a campus of wacky, suburban-style ranch houses. Point your camera out the window for some great landscapes. The **7 train** goes above ground during much of its run across the borough of Queens, ending up in Flushing, where a large proportion of the population is Chinese and Korean; the subway line has been affectionately dubbed the "Orient Express." The **C train**, too, is elevated during much of its journey from Harlem to the Washington Heights frontier.

One of my favorite subway journeys is on the **A train** in the Queens direction. The train crawls across the Broad Channel Causeway in the midst of the Jamaica Wildlife Refuge, then splits into two routes to traverse the Rockaway Peninsula — one goes to Far Rockaway while the other hits Rockaway Beach, made famous by the Ramones' song.

Even when the subway stays underground, it's a blast to ride. Aficionados position themselves at the extreme front or the extreme rear of the train to look out the single front- or back-facing window. There you can best admire the ancient tunnel architecture and the roller-coaster qualities of the ride.

For the most dedicated subway fans, there's the **Transit Museum** (Boerum Place and Schermerhorn Street, Brooklyn, 718-243-5839), spookily located underground in a disused spur of the old Court Street subway. You can get there underground via the R and N (Court Street Station), the A (Hoyt-Schermerhorn Station), or the 2, 3, or 4 (Borough Hall Station). The exhibit features old subway cars — some with wicker seats and leather straps — that you can crawl around in, motorman's apparel, turnstiles, and beautiful mosaics removed from renovated stations. They also have a nifty giftshop.

There's another subway line that most tourists never see that runs between the west side of Manhattan and several cities in New Jersey. Running on narrower-gauge tracks deep below the Hudson River, **PATH trains** can be caught on Avenue of the Americas at 32nd, 23rd, 14th, and 9th Streets, or at Christopher and Greenwich Streets in the West Village. This train goes on to make one stop in Hoboken and several in Jersey City. It connects at Journal Square with another PATH line that originates at the World Trade Center and zooms all the way to Newark, a city worth visiting on its own. This train also provides cheap connections to Newark Airport via cab or shuttle bus. The PATH trains are a bargain at $1, but the stations are unattended, so you'd better bring change or a crisp dollar bill.

SECRET

TAPAS

The craze peaked five years ago, but the tapas joints have continued to flourish and their numbers have increased by one or two every year. Maybe it's the earthy appeal of the food — small servings of Spanish standards like grilled chorizo, garlicky shrimp, toast smeared with olive paste, and shellfish in a savory sauce — or maybe it's just because you can make an evening of snacking and drinking in a single establishment. **Xunta** (174 First Avenue, 614-0620) is my favorite. It has a Galician orientation, which means that it serves up wedges of excellent, pie-shaped empanadas. Ñ (33 Crosby Street, 219-8856) is the darling of the Soho crowd, majoring in ports and sherries. For the well heeled, **Solera** (216 East 53rd Street, 644-1166) offers the broadest range of tapas in the bar, with a complete and expensive Spanish menu in the rear dining room. If total authenticity is what you desire, the meat district's **Rio Mar** (7 Ninth Avenue, 242-1623) predates the tapas fad, pumping out doctrinaire product in the downstairs bar, which is frequented by a number of oddball characters.

SECRET

TENEMENTS

When I was a kid in Minneapolis, my dad would stride into my messy room and declare, "This room looks like a tenement!" I didn't understand what he meant until I moved to New York and actually lived in one.

Tenements are multifamily dwellings first built in the mid-1800s by real-estate speculators intent on cramming as many people as possible into as small a space as possible. The first tenements had four floors with four apartments each; the rooms in each unit were laid out in a straight line, leading the dwellings to be called "railroad apartments." The interior rooms were without light or ventilation, and tenements rapidly became breeding grounds for squalor and disease. At their most overcrowded, these tenement apartments accommodated one extended family in each 10-by-10-foot room.

Around 1880, a tenement law was passed requiring that new buildings be constructed in the "dumbbell" style (the structures also became known as "old law" tenements), with a very narrow airshaft in the middle admitting air and small amounts of light into interior rooms. The impetus for the law was the rising number of tuberculosis cases, and the new arrangement actually did something to alleviate the conditions that transmit the disease. Twenty thousand dumbbell tenements were constructed over the next 20 years; today there are believed to be 200,000 tenement apartments remaining in various sections of the city.

Tenements are still home to many immigrants and those arriving from the Midwest and other parts of the United States. It's hard to imagine tenement life if you've never experienced it. The airshaft acts like a giant amplifier, and if you live in a six-story building (the legal limit for a residence with no elevator) with 24 apartments you can be sure to hear someone screaming at someone else, no matter what time of day it is. Bathtubs, an afterthought, were usually put in the kitchen, making privacy an issue. Often, two apartments share a single toilet stall in the common hallway.

To see rows of tenements still intact, stroll Orchard and the surrounding streets below Houston. And make a visit to the **Tenement**

Museum (90 Orchard Street, 421-0233), which has faithfully restored the apartments of several immigrant families from different eras within a single tenement. It offers a much richer insight into immigrant origins than a trip to the tourist trap of Ellis Island.

SECRET
THREE-CARD MONTE

❖

The game is played on a pile of cardboard boxes salvaged from a nearby trash can, and the game pieces are either three dog-eared playing cards or three white plastic bottle caps and a dried green pea. Also known as the shell game, this con has been in existence at least since the Middle Ages, and its ancient nature and tenacity in the streets of modern New York make it fun to watch.

But don't even consider playing, although you'll see many gullible people who will. Of the three cards, two are black and one is red. The monte dealer shows them to you so you know where the red one is, then rapidly slides the cards around the box top, inviting you to watch where the red one goes. It looks easy, and the bets escalate with the shouted encouragement of the dealer and the throng of spectators who have gathered to watch. The bet reaches $100, and you're sure you know where the red card is, but when your choice is turned over it's black and you've lost your money.

Here's how the con works: The dealer appears to be a lone entrepreneur, but in reality he has a crew of as many as 10 fellow criminals to assist him. Two or three are lookouts who position themselves on the same side of the street on the nearest corner and at the block's halfway point to watch for law enforcement. See if you can spot them. Typically, there will be another lookout or two much nearer the game to relay the warnings directly to the dealer, who is the leader. When you first spot the game, you'll typically see four or five players/spectators who seem to come from all walks of life. The dealer may be black, and a Mexican woman may step up to play. A thin white guy with a pock-marked face arrives a few minutes later. The dealer seems clumsy, almost drunk, and the Mexican woman easily wins $30, while the dealer seems a little embarrassed. Then the white guy steps up, and he, too, easily gets $50 from the dealer as an elderly Chinese woman watches, praising the white guy and defaming the dealer.

Everyone you see is an employee of the game, selected for their diverse ethnicity and acting skills; they give you a feeling of safety (How could these people possibly know each other?) and make the game seem easy to win. But when your turn comes and the bets increase, the dealer is now playing for real. The skilled dealers are world-class sharps who can palm cards and perform other sleight-of-hand tricks. Your chances of picking the red card are zero.

But some games lack a dealer who's a card whiz. In this case, you may actually win a round or two. But in this sort of game, you're likely to get mugged by the team's professional toughs as you depart. The point is, you can't win. But that doesn't mean you can't enjoy watching. These games depend on casual passersby to make the enterprise seem legitimate and provide a pool of suckers. You're in no danger if you observe and move on. The best place to find these games are in the blocks of West 14th Street on the southern side between Sixth and Eighth Avenues; in Harlem on 125th Street; and in the working-class shopping areas of Brooklyn and the Bronx. Look for the knot of people, the lookouts, and the pile of cardboard boxes.

SECRET

TRAMWAY

✤

Though this ain't the Alps, New York does have its own Swiss-made **aerial tramway**, which runs like a fine watch between the Upper East Side and Roosevelt Island from a terminal at Second Avenue and 60th Street. The cable car apogees at 250 feet in the air, and the $1.50 ride provides sweeping, incredible views of the East River. Information on the tram, which departs every 15 minutes between the hours of 6 A.M. and 2 A.M., can be had by dialing 832-4543. The attraction even has its own Web site: www.rioz.com.

Even though the tram originates in one of the more boring parts of Manhattan, **Roosevelt Island** itself is well worth a visit. Originally known as Blackwell's Island, and later Welfare Island, it was home to the city's almshouses, lunatic asylums, and tuberculosis sanitariums well into the twentieth century, but it's now a high-rise residential community devised on a utopian plan by Philip Johnson and John Burgee in the '70s. Nevertheless, some of the nineteenth-century structures persist in excellent condition, including a lighthouse at the northern end of the island designed by James Renwick Jr. in 1872, now preserved in a park flanked by weeping willows. It furnishes fine views of Hellgate, a stretch of tumultuous waters in the East River, the grave of many watercraft. A Web site (www.nyc 10044.com) provides the history of the island, related current events, and a delightful graphic of the tram car.

Bicycles are permitted on the tramway; they are a great way to get around the 1.75-mile-long island. You can also take the shuttle bus that leaves from the tram terminus (25¢) to the lighthouse and walk back.

SECRET

TRAVEL BOOKS

✤

Every Barnes & Noble and Borders bookstore has a prodigious travel section these days, but they can't hold a candle to the **Complete Traveller** (199 Madison Avenue, 685-9007), which boasts the most comprehensive collection of travel guides in the city and devotes an entire room to out-of-print travel volumes, many of which are fully illustrated and would be an asset to any coffee table. Prior to a recent trip to Havana, I found five guides to the city there and bought all of them, 'cause who can you trust?

As you might expect, Manhattan has several more stores devoted exclusively to vacation guides, including the three branches of the **Civilized Traveller** (2003 Broadway, 875-0306; 864 Lexington Avenue, 288-9190; and 2 World Trade Center, 786-0687), which also stock luggage and other accessories.

SECRET

TUSCAN

✤

Dozens of Tuscan-style restaurants have opened in the five boroughs over the last few years, emphasizing basic preparations and elemental flavors: foccacia and thin-crust pizza baked in wood-burning ovens, salads with arugula and goat cheese, roast chicken with rosemary. Virgin olive oil and balsamic vinegar spread like a miasma over everything.

My favorite Tuscan on the high end is **Follonico** (6 West 24th Street, 691-6359), serving complete dinners in the $40 range; on the low end are **Bar Pitti** (268 Sixth Avenue, 982-3300) and **Il Bagatto** (192 East 2nd Street, 228-0977), where you can get by for well under $20.

SECRET
TV DINNERS
❖

Lucky Cheng's (24 first Avenue, 473-0516) was the first — a pan-Asian restaurant whose most interesting feature was that the waitresses were really waiters. Though the food wasn't all that good, the shtick packed them in every night. Students brought their unsuspecting parents, couples came from Queens thinking this was what taking a walk on the wild side was all about, and connoisseurs of transvestitism, for whom Asian cross-dressers were an exotic treat, showed up. Predictably, there were imitators, of which **Lips** (2 Bank Street, 675-7710) is probably the best. The food quality here is a notch higher — the place offers mainly Italian fare, the dishes named after notorious New York drag queens like Joey Arias and Lypsinka. At $15 to $20, the entrees are expensive, but you have to consider that this also includes a floor show: the waitresses imitate pop stars and periodically break into song.

SECRET
TWENTY-FOUR HOURS
❖

To prove that New York is the city that never sleeps, here are a few places that are open around the clock (or almost).

Kang Suh (1250 Broadway, 564-6845), everybody's favorite Little Korea institution, is often more crowded at 4 A.M. than it is at the dinner hour. Patrons barbecue a selection of marinated meats tableside while picking at pan chan, an assortment of little pickled vegetable dishes that are served free of charge. Kang Suh's late-night constituency consists of Korean students returning from the clubs and vegetable-stand owners who are enjoying a traditional big breakfast before starting their business day. Kang Suh is one of the best places to awe visitors with the urbanity of the metropolis.

Other noteworthy 24-hour eateries include **Sarge's Deli** (548 Eighth Avenue, 679-0442) in Murray Hill, **Yaffa Café** (97 St. Marks Place, 674-9302) in the East Village, and **Florent** (69 Gansvoort Street, 989-5779) in the meat-packing district. Each has a fascinating late-night crowd. Of course, there are also the neon-lit hot-dog stands (see Secret Hot Dogs) if you need a quick late bite.

To practical matters: the discount drugstore **Duane Reade** at Sixth Avenue and Waverly is open 24 hours (674-5357), but the pharmacy part is, alas, only open till midnight. There's another Duane Reade at 91st Street and Broadway (799-3172) where the pharmacy is open all night. Three **Rite Aid** pharmacies also have all-night druggists (138 East 86th Street, 876-0600; 408 Grand Street, 529-7115; and 282 Eighth Avenue, 727-3854).

The main branch of the post office, **James A. Farley** (421 Eighth Avenue, 967-8585) is open all day and all night, and most postal services are available in the wee hours. **Kinko's Copy Shop**, with many branches in the city (consult the phone book), offers photocopying, computer rental, Fed Ex service, and so on. Incredibly, all branches are open round the clock. The **Home Depot** (550 Hamilton Avenue, Brooklyn, 718-832-8553) is open all the time to satisfy any late-night hardware or lumber needs that may arise, or you can just drop by to pick out a new pastel sink. Virtually any locksmith will provide late-night service — but often at staggering prices, so don't lose the key to those handcuffs!

To have roses delivered in the middle of the night, call **Not Just Roses** (247-6737). Then go relax at **Chelsea Billiards** (54 West 21st Street, 989-0096), secure in the knowledge that the joint never closes.

SECRET
UNITED NATIONS

For the thrill of crossing an international frontier without leaving the city, wander over to the **United Nations**. It's situated on a multiacre tract with beautiful views of the East River and Queens, including a huge Pepsi sign that dates to a time before Pepsi knew what Coke was. The first thing you should do is perambulate the formal gardens adjacent to the river, dotted with monumental sculpture, including a reworking of St. George and the Dragon called *Good Defeats Evil.* There's a sign with an arrow that says "Picnic Area," so I guess nobody will mind if you sit down and eat your lunch.

Eventually your steps will tend towards the complex of buildings designed by an international group, including Le Corbusier, Niemeyer, and Markelius, and completed between 1946 and 1963. The **Secretariat**, a huge glass tablet of a building, dominates the group, which sits around the main building as if admiring it; the second most prominent is the **General Assembly Building**, a low sweep of concrete. The '60s ambiance is one of the best reasons to hang

around the UN, where you still see guys with crew cuts, horn-rimmed glasses, and skinny ties. Just inside the visitors' door is a security check. You'll know you're on foreign soil because suddenly British English is the official language, with signs carrying odd spellings like "Programme" and "Centre." Next is an information desk manned by employees whose main function is to admit distinguished visitors (not including you or me) to less public parts of the building. You can skip it and head downstairs, where there's a series of gift shops, a post office, and an amazingly cheap cafeteria. Forego the burgers and foot-long hot dogs in favor of one of the Europe-leaning entrees, all priced under $6. The other day the choice was baked cod in a light cream-and-herb sauce, beef braised in wine with tons of vegetables, and a simple roasted half chicken, large enough to feed a family.

The gift shops are alternately fascinating and dumb. They offer craft items from nearly every country in the world at reasonable prices: Swiss music boxes, delicate Slovakian crystal, Malaysian heavy pewter (Malaysian?), dancing Thai dolls, Egyptian inlaid boxes, and china from China. Plenty of gourmet food items, too, and somber black-and-white postcards of former UN secretaries-general (quick, how many can you name?). One of the cheap thrills is the post office, where the cost of postage to any point in the US is exactly the same as it is in any other local post office, but the stamps you'll get are quite different; a UN postcard with a UN stamp and a UN cancellation makes a head-scratching conversation piece for your correspondant.

After your shopping spree, you might go upstairs and take the $7.50 tour, which includes the various meeting halls. It may provide you with a glimpse of one of the UN bodies in action, if you're very lucky (the General Assembly, for example, only meets three times a year). The tour takes about an hour and is offered in 12 languages.

In my opinion, you're better off just wandering around, although you'll have access to fewer places. The best way to blow money, however, is by gorging at the luncheon buffet in the **Delegates Dining Room**, where you'll be admitted if you have an advance reservation (963-9625) and are dressed "appropriately," which means no shorts or T-shirts. The buffet ($19.95, all you can eat) contains nearly 100 dishes reflecting the cooking styles of many nations. The food ranges from acceptable to quite good, but it can't match the panoramic view of the river.

SECRET
USED BOOKS

Hyping itself as "Seven Miles of Books," the **Strand** (828 Broadway, 473-1452) may be the world's largest source of used and remaindered volumes. Its dusty shelves, towering overhead, arranged in mazelike formation, give the place a gothic atmosphere. Finding a specific book can be a trial, but you're guaranteed to find something you want during the attempt. The Strand is also the number-one place to buy review copies of new books; they often arrive before the titles hit the bookstores, and the Strand sells them for half-price (the reviewers are paid 25%). In addition, there's a rare-book department that is particularly good for first editions of twentieth-century American literature.

Another favorite used-book spot is **Academy** (10 West 18th Street, 242-4848), which also carries "cut-out" CDs (review copies) at bargain prices.

SECRET
WALKING TOURS

✦

There's currently a mania for walking tours of the city conducted by cultural historians, authors, self-styled experts, and just plain crackpots. Typically, these tours are modestly priced, or even free, especially if sponsored by some organization with an ax to grind. Such tours are advertised via lamppost flyers and bulletin boards and by listings in the *Voice* (Open City), *New York* magazine (The Mix), and the *New York Press*. But the trend has snowballed, so that now the Fine Arts and Leisure section of the Friday *New York Times* has a comprehensive listing near the back called Spare Times. Here are a few regularly listed tours, with the phone numbers and sponsoring organizations. Call for times and to find out about other tours.

"Seinfeld and His Neighbors," a two-hour tour based on the popular television show set on the Upper West Side; $10, **Gotham Walk** (629-1886).

"Terminal City: The Grand Central Terminal," a complete once-over of the Beaux-Arts structure and its surrounding buildings; $15, sponsored by the **Municipal Arts Society** (935-3960).

"Historic Pubs and Taverns," 10 establishments, including the White Horse and Chumley's (see Secret Hidden Restaurants); $10, NYC **Discovery Tours** (465-3331).

"Multi-Ethnic Eating Tour," covering Chinatown, Little Italy, and the Jewish Lower East Side; $13, **Big Onion Walking Tours** (439-1090).

"Brooklyn Bridge Talk and Walk"; $10, sponsored by **Dr. Phil Walks and Talks** (888-377-4455).

"Vibrant Lincoln Square," including the Ansonia Hotel, which looks like it belongs in Paris, the Trump International Tower, and, of course, Lincoln Center; $5, **Adventures on a Shoestring** (265-2663).

"Grand Army Plaza and Park Slope," a tour of Brooklyn focusing on architecture in the area around Prospect Park; $25, **Beaux Arts Alliance** (639-9120).

"East Village Tales and Taverns," another tavern tour with literary aspects; $10 — which, they warn, doesn't include alcohol — **Street Smarts** (929-8262).

SECRET
WALL STREET
⚜

The financial district around Wall Street is a tourist mecca, but it's not one of the more interesting parts of town unless you're excited by the thought of huge amounts of money changing hands. Nevertheless, a tour of the stock exchange in not a bad way to while away a couple of hours. Once you get through the multimedia exhibit and arrive at the balcony above the trading floor things get exciting, particularly if you can identify the players on the floor according to the costumes they wear (paying attention during the preceding tour will help with this).

The **New York Stock Exchange** occupies a distinguished colonnaded structure at 20 Broad Street (656-5165), and the tours, offered from 9:15 till 2:45, are free. The catch is that the attraction is a popular one, so either arrive a little before 9 o'clock to get a ticket or prepare for long waits and possible disappointment. If you wash out at the New York Stock Exchange try the **American Stock Exchange** (86 Trinity Place, 306-1000), which also offers tours, and the action on the floor is just as exciting. Call to make an appointment. To experience a thrill of patriotic pride, make a brief visit to the **Federal Hall National Memorial** (15 Pine Street, 825-6888), a Greek Revival pile built in 1842 on the site of Washington's inauguration as the nation's first president. The exhibit inside is rather tepid, but it's free.

If you're the type who can plan things weeks in advance, call the **Federal Reserve Bank** (33 Liberty Street, 720-6130) to schedule a guided tour. They have a gold hoard that rivals that of Fort Knox; staring at it is the high point of the tour.

SECRET

WATCHES

❦

Lurking under scaffolds or in dark corners near **Times Square**, tall handsome Senegalese men open their attaché cases to tantalize passersby with a brief glimpse of their wares — watches labeled Rolex, Patek, and Cartier. As you might suspect, they're not the real thing, though made by talented craftspeople the *New York Times* once referred to as "the master watch forgers of Hong Kong." A little bargaining with these businessmen — who tend to be devout Muslims and are entirely on the up-and-up — yields prices of $10 or $15 per watch, and they keep pretty good time. The furtive nature of the transaction is a result of two things: the watches themselves are illegal knockoffs, and the vendors have no city license.

If you want to blow 200 times that amount or more on the real thing, try **Tourneau** (Madison Avenue and 52nd Street, 758-6098) or **Cartier** (653 Fifth Avenue, 753-0111). Or, for a price break on antique luxury, check out **Gregory Khmelnitsky** in the **Chelsea Antiques Building** (110 West 25th Street, 255-2056).

S E C R E T
WEB CAMS
⚜

Ever feel like thousands of people are watching you? Well, if you're standing on the corner of Third Avenue and 25th Street, they are! The city is filled with surveillance cameras — in banks, public buildings, and retail stores — but the latest addition to this voyeuristic onslaught is Web cams, video cameras that broadcast 24-hour-a-day live images of New York over the World Wide Web. Some of them are predictable — the cam on top of the **World Trade Center** (www.wtca.org/view.html), for example, that offers an almost envious view of the Empire State Building; or the three cameras on the 77th floor of the **Empire State Building** (www.realtech.com/webcam) that stare right back; or a dramatic view of the **Brooklyn Bridge** (www.romdog.com/bridge/brooklyn.html), as seen on the screen of a Macintosh PowerBook.

These views are nothing but gimmicky picture postcards. Much more interesting are the cameras that offer street-level views of the city, like the previously mentioned **Third and 25th cam** (www.videoeditor.com), or the one at **Fifth Avenue and 45th Street** (www.mte.com/webcam), which allowed me to watch one morning, enthralled, as a man whose face was hidden by a broad-brimmed hat approached the corner with a large package, and then meandered in and out of camera range for 15 minutes. He finally handed it off to a smartly dressed woman who headed north at a fast clip. Note that many live sites must be actively refreshed by clicking on the reload button of your browser, and that some browsers do not support all Web cams — if one doesn't work for you, try another.

Most amazing of all is the **France Telecom Web site** (www. francetel.com:8080), located at Rockefeller Center, which allows to you to select from among six cameras and then manipulate them with your own computer — pointing, zooming, and focusing. When you find an image you like, it may be saved as a "postcard" that can then be sent to friends over the Internet. Much better than an actual visit to Rockefeller Center, believe me.

SECRET

WILLIAMSBURG

❖

No, we're not talking about colonial Williamsburg, the Revolution-ary-era tourist trap in Williamsburg, Virginia — we're talking about Brooklyn's Williamsburg, a hip tourist trap of more recent vintage, located across the Williamsburg Bridge from Manhattan. When the East Village became yuppified 10 years ago, this is the neighborhood that absorbed the brunt of the exodus, becoming a bohemian paradise almost overnight. But while the East Village housed its artistic masses and hangers-on in six-story tenements (see Secret Tenements), Williamsburg offered postindustrial lofts and two-story frame townhouses; here the typical hipster apartment is located just upstairs from the Polish landlady. That took some getting used to.

Now **Bedford Street** (the first stop on the L train from Manhattan) is chock-a-block with coffeehouses, art-supply stores, galleries, boutiques, and trendy, inexpensive restaurants, interspersed with relatively ancient Polish butcher shops and cafés. It makes a fascinating panorama. The boho influx has now extended to the second and third stops on the L (Lorimer/Metropolitan and Graham, respectively), comprising historically Italian and Puerto Rican neighborhoods.

A few of the neighborhood's highlights: Everyone (including staid *New York* magazine) is talking about **Galapagos** (70 North 6th Street, 718-782-5188), the new nightclub/performance space/wine bar located in a former mayonnaise factory, the huge metal vats of which are still visible. Call to see whether a particular evening features a film series, musical performance by house band Vaimarama, theater piece, or retro-punk conceptual-art shocker, like a man in jockey shorts running a razor blade over his torso. As David Byrne says, "This ain't no disco."

But most of Williamsburg's night scene is more bucolic, consisting of impromptu musical events at the **Charleston** (174 Bedford Avenue, 718-782-8717), a pizzeria that presents many of Williamsburg's country-inflected hometown acts in its adjacent dingy bar. A similar music scene is fostered at **Teddy's** (96 Berry Street, 718-384-9787), an antideluvion bar that serves decent hamburgers. Music is also offered at **Wet Paint** (124 North 6th Street, 718-599-5576), where the Italian food is not so great, and at a number of fly-by-night underground clubs (which may or may not be open when you read this), like **Dirty Deeds** (97 South 6th Street, 718-486-6277) and the subterranean **Rubuland** (141 South 5th Street, 718-782-8523), where mock-professional wrestling is featured.

During the last five years, the nabe has evolved into a dining destination as well. Anchoring the scene is **Plan Eat Thailand** (184 Bedford Avenue, 718-599-5758), one of the city's best and cheapest Thai restaurants, where you'll have to wait in line to get a table most evenings; and the quizzically named **Oznot's Dish** (79 Berry Street, 718-599-6596), where artfully mismatched crockery and a bistro menu with North African/Mexican/Middle Eastern overtones are the attractions. To plumb the neighborhood's older ethnic heritage, visit **Bamonte's** (32 Withers Street, 718-384-8831), since 1900 the home of luscious, tomato-kissed food from the Campania region of Italy dished up in a setting that hasn't changed much since Frank Sinatra's childhood. Other neighborhood faves are the centrally located **Mugs Ale House** (125 Bedford Avenue, 718-384-8494) and **Miyako** (243 Berry Street, 718-486-0837), serving Korean and Japanese food.

SECRET
WITCHCRAFT

❧

The Wiccans are out there, but they keep a low profile. There's **Magickal Childe** (35 West 19th Street, no phone), a store with a fascinating collection of books, incense, candles, ritual robes, and texts, plus a wall of shelves containing over 300 kinds of herbs in dusty jars inscribed with such names as "gall of the earth," "devil's claw," "feverfew," and "life everlasting." There are also Aleister Crowley posters, talismen (or should it be talispersons?), and daggers with wavy blades, bargain priced at $22.50. The store's bulletin board is a good place to find services offered to, and by, witches and warlocks. On it there's a notice, for example, of the Satanic mass offered every Saturday at 1 A.M. on Manhattan Cable channel 57.

Stores selling similar merchandise include **Enchantments** (341 East 9th Street, 228-4394) in the East Village, in whose backyard garden the Minoan Sisterhood celebrates festivals — new initiates are welcome — and **Morgana's Chamber** (242 West 10th Street, 243-3415), a new shop in the West Village. The latter supplies a very ambitious list of on-premises classes with titles like Magickal Incense Making, Runes, Kitchen Witchery, and Wicca 101.

S E C R E T

WORLD MUSIC

⚘

The term "world music" has come to designate international acts that deliver hyped, overpriced performances covered by every periodical in town. But go back a few years to the origins of world music — ethnographic musicians from the four corners of the Earth traveling on shoestring budgets and playing small venues like churches and colleges. That spirit is still alive at the pioneering **World Music Institute** (49 West 27th Street, 545-7536, Web site: www.heartheworld.org), which for 14 years has presented the best in international music in intimate settings and classical-music concert halls. Ticket prices run as low as $10, and recent programs, which often occur at the rate of three per week, include the Aboriginal music of Australia, flamenco, Persian and Indian improvisational music, Turkish whirling dervishes, Korean dancers, and a program of Afro-Cuban ensembles.

SECRET
ZINES
⚜

Fanzines, affectionately known as "zines," are small-circulation homemade publications that usually focus on one narrow field of endeavor. Originally, this field was uniformly rock music, often one particular band, but gradually the zine world came to encompass nearly every type of interest or undertaking, from cooking, to sex, to jazz, to riot grrrls, to punk, to New Age spirituality, to obscure collecting obsessions. Zines are a distinctly Downtown phenomenon, and the retailer with the largest selection is **See Hear** (59 East 7th Street, 505-9781), which sells almost nothing but fanzines. The proprietor is an avid civil libertarian, so you'll find many publications that might be considered downright illegal in other cities. The bible of the fanzine, available at the store, is *Factsheet5* ("your perpetually surprising guide to the zine revolution"), published every four months and containing hundreds of reviews. See Hear maintains a Web site (www.zinemart.com) that provides a catalog and ordering info, but it's much more fun to browse in person. A slimmer selection of zines is also available at **Tower Books** (383 Lafayette Street, 228-5100).

THE SECRET FUTURE

No tour guide can be definitively comprehensive, especially when the aim is to uncover those hidden places that have previously escaped notice. Undoubtedly, some worthwhile attractions have remained hidden even from our best efforts to ferret them out.

In the interest of our own self-improvement, we ask readers to let us know of the places they've unearthed that they believe warrant inclusion in future editions of *Secret New York*. If we use your suggestion, we'll send you a free copy on publication. Please contact us at the following address:

Secret New York
c/o ECW PRESS
2120 Queen Street East, Suite 200
Toronto, Ontario, Canada M4E 1E2

Or e-mail us at: ecw@sympatico.ca

PHOTO SITES

SUBJECT INDEX

Books and Literary Interests

Child's Play

Ethnic Eating

Resources and References

Restaurants

Sacred Spaces

ALPHABETICAL INDEX